BUSINESS MANAGEMENT FOR SOLICITORS

Turning your practice into a business

by

David S Porter

and

Vanessa J Openshaw

© David S Porter and Vanessa J Openshaw 2001

Published by
EMIS Professional Publishing Ltd
31–33 Stonehills House
Welwyn Garden City
Hertfordshire
AL8 6PU

ISBN 1 858 11 274 5

All rights reserved. No part of this publication may be reproduced, stored in a retrieval system, or transmitted, in any form or by any means, electronic, mechanical, photocopying, recording or otherwise, without the prior permission of the publisher.

The moral right of the authors has been asserted.

Typeset by Saxon Graphics Ltd, Derby.

Cover design by Jane Conway.

Printed and bound in the UK by Intype,
Elm Grove, Wimbledon, SW19 4HE.

CONTENTS

Acknowledgements vii

Introduction 1

Chapter 1

Pricing 7

- Time costing
- Law Society's recommendations
- The realities in the market place
- Back to basics: the Barrow Boy
- Application of the principles to a solicitor's office
- The cost of running departments and the true profit
- Accountability of fee-earners and partners

Chapter 2

Forecasting and budgeting 21

- Understanding the "shape" of the business
- Expenses: fixed and variable costs
- Considering other expenses; identifying fixed costs and variable costs with resultant margins; including a notional salary for partners
- How the fees are made up; bottom up; and the effect of time costing
- Bidding for variable costs: temporary staff; training; marketing; and library
- Extrapolating the results to assess the margins

Chapter 3

Cash flow   **43**

- Monthly analysis of fees by departments and branches
- Monthly analysis of expenses on the same basis
- Preparation of cash flow allowing for "cash" receipts, and VAT
- Consequence of forecasts on overdraft drawings and expenses

Chapter 4

The balance sheet, profit and loss account and taxation under self-assessment   **63**

- Fixed assets
- Current assets
- Creditors; taxation, VAT and overdraft
- Net current liabilities
- Financed by: capital accounts and drawings for partners
- Notes to the accounts

Chapter 5

Computers   **81**

- Computers: definitions
- Wordprocessing and spreadsheets
- Nerworking
- Internet and dedicated systems

Chapter 6

Management, staff and teams   **95**

- Management structure for partners, staff and teams
- Managing departments and people
- Investors, Lexcel accreditation generally and monitoring activities
- Franchise and best practice
- Appraisals: partners and staff

Chapter 7
Strategic planning and analyzing performance   **113**

- Strategic meeting
- Setting the plan
- Business analysis: Strengths, Weaknesses, Opportunities and Threats
- Setting goals

Chapter 8
Marketing   **123**

- Activating the strategic plan
- Internal organisation
- Marketing mix
- Promotional activities

Chapter 9
Mergers   **139**

- Types and budget requirement
- Comparing the practices and culture
- Asking awkward questions
- The net worth of partners; real value of debtors; disbursements outstanding; work in progress
- Property
- Accounting methods, taxation and pensions
- Communicating change

Chapter 10
The future   **151**

- Historical perspectives
- Growth and shape
- Core business
- Likely changes

Further Reading   **161**

Index   **165**

Tables

1	Balance sheet	34
2	Office expenses	36
3	Department budgets	37
4	Corporate budget	38
5	Administration budget	39
6	Forecast of fees received after VAT discounted by 5% for cash	46
7	Forecast actual and projected fees	47
8	Forecast actual and projected expenses	50
9	Cash flow forecast	52

ACKNOWLEDGEMENTS

Having started this venture in 1975 it is gratifying to get a fifth edition. There have been many changes since the first edition not least that the profession has now to operate as a business.

We are also grateful for the assistance given to us by Kim Carmillie in the chapter on computers. Andrew Griffin has been an inspiration for taking the book on. James Griffin has gone over the text with a fine tooth-comb and made many helpful suggestions.

The ideas expressed in the have been developed over the last 25 years from experience in a growing practice.

INTRODUCTION

Ask a commercial solicitor to identify the essential points in a commercial lease and he can reel them off without thinking about them. Ask a litigator to explain the procedures under Woolf and he will do so without too much effort. Ask either of them what the net margin in their department is and they will tell you to ask the in-house accountant. What is more, they will even go as far as to say it isn't their problem. The reason is not hard to find. Solicitors by and large spend all their formative years learning the law. They do not have time in eight years of study to learn the business. As a result they sometimes fail to understand even the most basic of concepts. The purpose of this book is to encourage solicitors to look at their practices as businesses. This does not mean that they have to abandon their core values or stop looking after the clients, it merely means that to carry out their work efficiently and to the best advantage of their clients they must have a feel for how their business works.

There are a myriad of books on business management from the frankly incomprehensible to the facile. It is intended that this book will be a practical introduction of the basic principles involved in running any type of business, and will be applicable to solicitors whether they are working in private practice, industry, local authorities or public bodies. The principles are common to all types of business and are well tried and tested and do work. Their application, however, is much more complex. Solicitors must stand back from their practices (or departments) and recognise that they are businesses like all other businesses.

SHAPE

It is for that reason that solicitors have to be aware of the environment in which they work and have a feel for the shape of the business. It is difficult to define the idea of "shape" but it will become apparent as the book progresses that all business have a fundamental shape which dictates how they behave.

It is essential that solicitors have a feel for that "shape" so that they can know when thinks are going wrong and are able to do something about it. How can one get a feel for the "shape" of your business? Only by thoroughly understanding how it works. To be a successful sailor you must have a feel for the boat. There are a lot of variables. For a start the wind or lack of it dictates the amount of sail you need, and the way in which you balance the boat. It also matters if you are going into the wind or away from it. If you are trying to get the boat to sail into the wind, everything has to be tight, and in a heavy swell you must lean out. You lean out to keep the boat upright because it sails best in that position. Then there are the sails. When should you have the mainsail full up? Should you have the jib at the front loose or tight? What about the spinnaker? You can sail a boat on your own, with one crew member, or in the larger racing boats with a large number of crew.

It doesn't matter how big or small the yacht, the same rules apply. If you know the rules you can make a fairly good job of sailing. With a little practice you could get to sail fairly well and could sense when there was a shift in the wind. You obviously need to sail the yacht as efficiently as possible, without tiring yourself. Your boat is unique and has its own idiosyncracies; other boats of different dimensions are different to handle, and you will need to adjust accordingly.

Sailing is not unlike running a business. Fee income varies in a twelve-month period quite dramatically, like the wind. On the yacht you don't gear up for maximum wind, if you get too much you either release the sails to let some out or risk capsizing. If it's blowing too hard you don't go out at all or you get a stronger boat. Similarly, if the fees are rising, you take on staff to help; if they dry up, you have to make redundancies. Like sailing, however, you have to anticipate the squalls and lulls, that you can see on the water which might be going to affect you. If you know what your boat is capable of you know what you can take on. If you don't, you sink! Similarly, if the office is not set up correctly and you haven't made some intelligent guesses as to the way the wind is blowing, you could go bust. With some experience you get to sense what might happen and take the appropriate action.

So what is the shape of a particular business? Clearly there is no point in investing in a business if it is not going to make you any money. To make money it must at least cover the running costs and provide a reasonable wage for you, including a return on the capital you have employed in the business. Let us take a simple example of a young solicitor who wants to start up as a conveyancer. He might decide that the shape would look something like this:

INTRODUCTION

	£
Anticipated fees, say 375 houses at an average of £250 per matter =	93,750

Expenses

	£	
Rent of small office	7,500	
Heating, lighting, rates	2,750	
Fixtures and fittings on lease	4,200	
Telephone, stationary, postage	5,700	
Solicitors Indemnity Fund	7,200	
Staff	24,000	
Miscellaneous expenditure	5,500	56,850
Gross profit		36,900
Less the salary he might be able to earn elsewhere		24,500
Net profit		12,400
Margin		13.23%

On these figures he will make a super profit of £12,400. This represents the return that he makes for the effort and anxiety he puts into the business and amounts to 13.23% of turnover. He will in addition make his wage of £24,500. It must be recognized however that he won't be paid all at once. Solicitors are notorious for not collecting their debts, and are often prepared to wait 120 days or more before they are paid. In the above example this would represent £30,822 (£93,750/365 to give the value per day, i.e. £256.85 × 120.)

Unless he takes into account all the commercial considerations, the solicitor will never realize what the shape of his business is, nor how to organize it to his best advantage.

HOW THIS BOOK IS ARRANGED

Each chapter will have worked examples which are taken from a set of figures (tables within the text), and will also pose questions which require answers in relation to your own business.

CHAPTER 1

This suggests ways in which solicitors can arrive at what they should charge. This can be on a time basis or be related to the volume and type of work involved. There are realities in the market place, however, which can fundamentally alter the amount that might be recovered. Time costing is reduced to a management tool – where it should have been long ago as suggested by one of the authors of this book in his first edition in 1976!

CHAPTER 2

This puts into perspective the fees that a solicitor might expect to charge by completing a forecast and budget that realistically represents what might be achieved. However good the forecasting and budgetary process, it is unlikely to be absolutely accurate. It is going to be wrong. It is therefore essential that the results are monitored so that adjustments can be made to the plan.

CHAPTER 3

This deals with the lubricating of the budget by the injection of the appropriate amount of cash. If an accurate cash flow statement is not completed, it is likely that the practice will run out of money. As a result of the cash flow projection it may be necessary to go back to the forecast and budget to fine-tune it to fit in with the realities of the cash generated.

CHAPTER 4

This works through a balance sheet showing how all the various figures relate to and interact with each other. For example, if drawings remain the same and the profit reduces then the overdraft goes up and the capital accounts come down.

CHAPTER 5

This addresses the revolution in computers and the Internet. Most firms of solicitors are spending substantial sums of money on computers, but most have not worked out the cost savings (if any) nor the benefit in bottom-line profit to the firm.

CHAPTER 6

This deals with the most important part of any office, the management of staff and teams. Solicitors are, by and large, poor listeners particularly where staff are concerned. They do not recognise that their workforce is crucial to the running of the office and they often fail to communicate properly. Accreditation – in the form of Investors in People, Lexcel, ISO 9000 and the franchise – go a long way to redress the balance. In the longer term they may be a "given" without which work will not be attainable.

CHAPTER 7

This deals with setting a strategic plan, its preparation and implementation. If the partners do not know where their business is going it is unlikely that anyone else will. There needs to be a clear focus if the business is not to drift. It is essential that everyone buys into the strategy. This can lead to distressing considerations if the decision is that certain types of work might reduce or even disappear altogether. Once the strategy is decided the rest of the management considerations flow from it.

CHAPTER 8

This deals with the concept of marketing. Marketing is the way in which the strategic plan is brought to life. Marketing is not advertising and it needs a long time to take effect. It is about positioning the firm in the marketplace within the terms of the strategic plan so that the right clients are attracted to the business to make the forecast profit.

CHAPTER 9

This looks at some of the advantages and disadvantages of merging. It is possible to grow organically, which has the benefit of keeping the existing culture. It could be, however, that faster growth is needed than can be achieved organically.

CHAPTER 10

This draws together all the ideas addressed in the book and attempts to make a judgment as to where the business of the law might be going.

PUTTING THE THEORY INTO PRACTICE

This book will show you how to apply good accounting principles to your own organization. By establishing its "shape" and making sure you understand these basic, sensible rules, you will be able to ensure that the business side of your firm will operate smoothly and profitably. That frees you up to carry on being good legal practitioners…!

CHAPTER 1
PRICING

"I can't tell you how much it will cost because I don't know how long it's going to take, but you will get a professional job professionally done!"

"Why don't you contact a few other solicitors and ring me last?"

The above represents two extremes of the way in which solicitors have been known to quote prices for their clients. Neither takes into account how much it would cost the practice to complete the work, nor how much the client was prepared to pay. Pricing in any discipline is a great skill and solicitors have been ambushed over the years by time costing and recently by a much more sophisticated market place.

HISTORICAL OVERVIEW

Prior to 1972 much of the legal work in provincial practices was conveyancing driven, litigation being a poor relation. The profession was nicely cocooned against the market place because all conveyancing work was based on a fixed scale. Litigation did not have the benefit of a scale fee, although the level of the scale in property transactions helped as a guide for litigious fees. An example of the haphazard pricing methods of the 1970s was when a local solicitor seriously suggested that the amount he should receive for a litigious matter ought to be based on the size of the file! In fact the solicitor held up the file and said "Compared to a conveyancing matter where I received £500, this file must be worth £1,500!"

The profession as a whole was making very good money and, up to that time, very few clients would have dreamed of arguing about their solicitor's bill. That bill consisted of a scale fee for conveyancing work and an additional fee for the work in relation to a mortgage. As the cost of all the work was more than covered by the conveyancing fee, the mortgage work added about 25% to the profit. Part of the justification for such a high figure was as 'insurance' against future claims of negligence. In 1974/5 the housing market started to collapse. At the same time more people had qualified as solicitors and as a result clients were shopping around to see if they could obtain a reduction in the fees. The profession took the view that the removal of the scale fee would make competition easier.

At that time very few solicitors bothered to prepare budgets and forecasts and certainly had very little concern about cash flows and overdrafts. As a direct result they did not have any idea of the cost of running their practices and they were therefore totally unable to assess whether the loss of scale fees would fundamentally affect their businesses.

In an attempt to produce some guidance the Law Society suggested to solicitors that, as time was the only constant they could measure in their practices, they should base their charges on the productive time available to them. They suggested that a solicitor could reasonably expect to work for 1,125 productive hours each year. They then produced a formula which showed how much the solicitors would have to charge to cover the expenses of the practice before they made something for themselves. This calculation produced the "expense rate" for the firm. As solicitors needed to make a profit, they had to add a percentage (known as a "mark up") to that expense rate, which resulted in the hourly rate they should charge to their clients to achieve their forecast profit. This was called the "charge-out rate". The mark up could be anything from 25% to 50% although the usual mark-up was 25%.

In working out the amount of profit that a practice should try to achieve, it was suggested that 33% of the turnover should cover the wages of the staff, a further 33% should cover the rest of the expenses, which left a further 33% for profit. The expense of time calculation included a "notional salary" for the partners. The logic for this was that a partner could expect to work for somebody else at a market rate. As a result the partners were only making a profit if they received further amounts above that figure. This truly represented the reason for working for themselves and gave a return for all the effort and risk involved in running the practice.

It is some indication as to how things have slipped that a margin, for "super profit" (after allowing for notional salaries) of 15% is probably a good average in most practices these days.

The mistake which the Law Society made was to indicate that this method of calculation would produce a fairly standardized charge for all firms across the country – not unlike the old scale. What they did not recognize, and what the profession has still not recognized, is that the client may not necessarily agree to the "charge out rate"! After all, time costing is a calculation to identify how much a firm should charge to achieve the desired profit. The figures are worked out in-house and may bear no relationship to what some, or all, of the clients are minded to pay. If the clients refuse to pay on this basis then the partners must look at the market place and amend their aspirations. Where clients will pay more, then the partners could increase the fees. This is a marketing and sales exercise and is discussed in more detail in Chapter 8.

In spite of the in-house figures being produced by time costing, with experience, those figures should fit into the market place in which the firm operates. The level of fee will depend on where the practice wishes to be in the market place.

For example, the legal aid charge on green form advice can never be anything more than a basis from which to obtain work paying at a better level. After all if the rate charged to the client is only £45 per hour, when the fee earner's rate to the practice is £112 per hour, the work produces a loss of £67 per hour. This is below many break even figures which are discussed later and no amount of volume will ever put that right. The practice would need to decide why it offered to do green-form work. The only reason can be that it leads to other work which can be charge out at a proper rate. The reduction in fee of £67 represents a discount. Unless that discount is recovered elsewhere, the desired profit of the practice is not going to be achieved.

It could be argued therefore that there is no point in recording time if the practice is to charge at a rate which it cannot alter. That assumption would be incorrect. If the practice knows that an hour of green-form advice creates a loss of £67, then they know that the same fee earner on £112 will have to make £179 per hour on another job (£67 plus his usual rate of £112); or some other part of the office must make good the shortfall. If that cannot be achieved then the partners must either settle for less, or must stop doing green-form work. They could, for example, use less expensive staff, or perhaps a computer system. There may be repercussions for the partner or fee earner who does the green-form work, as they will have to find other work to do to achieve their target. If they cannot do so then they may well have to leave the practice, as they cannot sensibly be carried indefinitely.

The other extreme for time costing might be a takeover at £3,750,000. The time of the commercial partner at say £225 per hour could amount to 75 hours to complete the work. He would probably be working in a team so the example is a little over simplified, but it will make the point. It could be that the takeover has to be completed within a very tight time scale, where the consequences of success are a substantial tax saving to the proprietors. The partner's rate of £225 per hour for 75 hours would produce £16,875. Three quarters of one per cent of £3,750,000 on the other hand produces £28,125. The client might be content to work on a percentage as it gives him a finite figure for his own budget and he recognizes that the matter has to be handled professionally. A mark up of 60% of the time would be very acceptable to the practice.

Both the above examples are extremes and it would be foolish to use them as a reason for not using time costing. They both demonstrate the real cost to the practice of the work compared to the forecast, from which useful conclusions can be drawn. If, however, the practice carries out the proposals suggested in this book they should have a fairly accurate idea of what they might expect. It will be seen how in-house time costing can be used to maximize performance and more importantly to monitor results. So how should solicitors price their work? We suppose the answer is that they should go back to basics and understand some of the principles of running a business.

THE WAY FORWARD

Perhaps the best example of a basic business model is that of the barrow boy selling his fruit. He knows how much he paid for his barrow; he knows the cost and amount of the various fruits he has on the barrow; he also knows the return he wants to produce to make it worth him getting out of bed in the morning. Let us suppose the figures for the day appear as below:

					£
A	Proposed turnover on a 33% break point				80.00
B	Cost of barrow to be met out of sales today			2.07	
C	Cost of fruit	410 apples at 4p	16.40		
		500 bananas at 5p	25.00		
		320 pears at 3p	9.60	51.00	53.07
D	Profit (33% of £80 = £26.40) Margin (approx 33%)				26.93
E	Notional wage				20.00
F	Super profit				6.93
G	Super profit margin				8.66%

Our entrepreneurial barrow boy has just gone into business, he has an interest free loan from a family member of £500, that he intends to pay off in the first year. He intends to work five days a week, which works out at 241 days in the year taking three weeks holiday and anticipating a week off sick (365 – 104 – 20 days = 241)

A is the projected turnover if the business is to have a profit of 33% of that turnover.

B is the daily cost of the barrow which he wishes to pay for in 12 months and for which he has borrowed (£500/241 = £2.07 per day). This is a fixed cost as he cannot carry out the work without his barrow.

C is the cost of fruit which is his raw materials. This is a variable cost as he can buy more or less depending on the seasonal availability and the local demand.

D is his profit (called "contribution" or "gross profit" in business without notional salaries). This is the difference between the price he buys at, the cost of his barrow and the amount he charges his customers. He expects to make a daily profit of £26.93. Where a person is running his own business then anything over the costs of the business belongs to him and at this point, for the purposes of this exercise, is treated as profit. His profit margin is 33% of turnover.

E is his notional wage. This represents what he thinks he could earn on the day if he worked a barrow for somebody else. It is arguable that, until he has made that amount of money, there is very little point in him working for himself.

F is his super profit. This represents a return on his investment and effort, which he would not receive if he worked for somebody else and is to the nearest whole number 9% of his turnover. Whether this is the right percentage or not depends on how other barrow boys do.

The advantage to the barrow boy in working the market is that he knows exactly where he is all the time. He has 1,230 pieces of fruit to sell. If he sells them at an average price of 6.5p, he will achieve his turnover (1,230 × 6.5p = £79.95). He also knows that, when he has sold 817 pieces of fruit at that rate, he will then have covered his costs of £53.10 (817 × 6.5p = £53.10). Anything he makes thereafter will be profit. If he makes no more he will have "broken even". His break-even point is very important to him. Until he achieves this he cannot afford to reduce his price, because any discount means he is not covering his costs. Once he has achieved break even, he can alter the price up or down depending on what he wants to achieve. If it is a sunny day and there are plenty of potential customers, he can afford to put his prices up, confident that he will sell all his fruit. If it is raining or getting to the end of the day and his stock is going off, he will reduce his price to get rid of it. The example is over simplistic but it makes the point that, until you know what your break even is, it is impossible to fix a price.

Further, if the shape of the business changes then the mathematics changes. The shape is dictated by the relationship between turnover, expenses and bottom-line profit. If the turnover goes up and expenses remain the same, the profit goes up. Conversely, if expenses go up and the turnover remains the same, the profit goes down. The trick is to get the right balance, so that the work can be done efficiently to produce the best profit. For example, if the barrow boy becomes ambitious and decides that he wants to earn £50 per day, then his profit must go up by approximately £23.97. If he is to keep the shape right then his turnover would have to go to £151 (33% of £151 = £49.83, say £50). To achieve £151, this represents an increase on his selling price of nearly double the 6.5p to 12p (1,260 × 12p = £151 approximately). If that is the position he must either increase his volume at the old price to achieve sales of 2,323 (£151/6.5p); or stock more expensive fruit which would justify the higher price; or change his location to a potentially wealthier area. He will need to know his market place well if he is to be successful.

No businesses have any excuse for not knowing either their market place nor their shape. This automatically includes knowing the profit and break evens not only by department but also by product or fee income.

Now let us consider how this translates into an average solicitor's practice. What tends to matter these days in the everyday hurly-burly of practice is that individual fees are kept as high as possible, by whatever means. Fees in excess of £250,000 and rising to £750,000 or more in the very large practices are normal. Even in medium practices fees in the £120,000 to £190,000 range are usual. Practices are tending to specialize more and more, so that the individual partner or fee earner only knows about his or her part of the business. Even though computerised results are available, most fee earners and partners only want to know whether their fees are keeping up to target. As the profession has had very little training in business management few solicitors have the barrow boy's skills. Certainly they would have difficulty in identifying their break even either by department or individually. The difficulty with this is that fee income is relentlessly pursued without necessarily inquiring whether any profit is being made. After all, fees of £275,000 three quarters of the way through the year might help one's ego at partners meetings, but if it has cost £280,000 to achieve there would seem to be little point in doing the work at all. Perhaps that is why solicitors tend not to look at their actual contribution to profit. Those who do achieve good profit margins feel contented with what they do. Those who do not, keep their heads down, in the hope that nobody will ask them difficult questions. The problem is that the fee earner making the largest fees is somehow treated differently from the rest.

> "What ever you do – don't upset George – he's the biggest fee earner you know!"

It would be worth looking at George's contribution to the super profit. A closer examination of his fees may well reveal not only that he takes the best work for himself, which might more appropriately be done by another fee earner, but also that he is given credit for fees, part of which ought to be credited to other fee earners. Even if those figures are not deducted it might be that secretarial assistance including other clerks is such that his contribution to profit is actually very little. If you add in his share of overhead costs, to his share of the office expenses and the wages of people in his department and deduct the total from his fees for the same period, he may well be carrying out the work at a loss. It certainly would be important to find out!

There may be all sorts of reasons why departments are under- or over-achieving, but the practice needs to know. After all there is little point in having sophisticated information if nobody takes any notice of it, or perhaps cannot fully understand it. It is essential that each fee earner, partner and department understands how the fees and expenses impact on the overall profit. On the face of it the fees should be fairly straightforward. If, however, individual fees are broken down, it might be found that some of them stray into other disciplines or departments. The excuse will be that the fee earners were acting for special clients or friends, who would otherwise have taken the work elsewhere. The truth of the matter is that the additional work bolsters up the solicitors' fees so that they achieve target.

Even more common is entering bills on to the system, particularly at the year end, even though the bills are not going to be delivered to the client for sometime, let alone be paid! The effect of this across a large number of fee earners and partners is to give an artificial picture of the gross income which is not backed up by hard cash, because the fees have not been paid.

What the people in the departments need to know are the costs of running the department and their contributions to the profit or bottom line. If that is going to be achieved, it is essential that the partners understand the shape of the various departments and the office as a whole. If a business is to run on the traditional 33% profit margin, it has an inescapable shape. The basic principles apply to all business.

Let us take a small conveyancing practice, as this is a simple model to underline the principles. Let us suppose that a young solicitor setting up on her own would settle for an income of £33,000 per year from residential conveyancing. The proposed shape of her business means that £33,000 is 33% of her turnover. This means she must turn over £100,000, as 33% of £100,000 is £33,000. If a 33% margin means she makes a profit of £33,000 then she will have £67,000 available to run the office.

	£	£
Her desired turnover is		100,000
Her expenses are, say		
Wages		
Secretary	13,000	
General office	10,000	
Telephonist	10,000	
	33,000	
Expenses		
Rent and rates	6,500	
Light and heat	1,600	
Telephone	2,400	
Postage	4,200	
Stationery	1,600	
Books	800	
Insurance	1,200	
Equipment leasing	2,750	
Accountancy	1,200	
Indemnity insurance	7,750	
Car	1,500	
Bad debts	800	
Training CPD	700	
Advertising	1,000	34,000	67,000
Net profit		33,000
Notional salary		25,000
Super profit		8,000
Percentage of turnover		8%

Her break even would be £67,000. At break even, of course, like the barrow boy, she makes nothing for herself, but she will cover her expenses. She needs to know what her break even is, if she is to charge her clients on a proper basis.

The trouble is that a conveyancing practice is slightly more sophisticated than a barrow boy's. She needs a simple way of working all this out. There is no doubt that the one measurable asset she has is her time. Some of this she will use merely to run her office, the balance ought to be available to service clients. On that basis she should to be able to work for 1,125 productive hours in any one year.

This figure is made up as follows.

PRICING

Hours in day	9 to 5 with one hour for lunch	7 hours	
	Admin and miscellaneous time	2 hours	
	Productive hours available for charging	5 hours	
	Hours in a week, 5 × 5	25	
	Hours available, 52 × 25		1300
	less Holidays (20 days at 5 hours)	100	
	Sickness (5 days at 5 hours)	35	
	Training (8 days at 5 hours)	40	175
	Productive hours available in year		1,125

From her budget she wants to turn over £100,000. If she works 1,125 hours she must charge £88.89, say £90, per hour (£100,000/1,125). As long as she can record her time satisfactorily she can readily identify the time she spends on each client. Suppose, for example, that the average conveyance takes three hours, she would need to charge £270 to achieve her target (£90 × 3 = £270). Whether she could charge that or not would depend on the price of the property being dealt with. The average price of a house in England is between £75,000 and £90,000. £270 only represents 0.36% of that price. Given that estate agents consistently charge 1.5%, that does not look out of the way. Unfortunately, buyers at this level take an 80% or 90% mortgage. Let us suppose that our solicitor is acting for somebody buying a house at £85,000. A mortgage of 90% would represent £76,500 of the price. This means that the buyer is contributing £8,500 to the price. The buyer would also need to spend more money on top of that for removals, furnishings and there may be alterations.

The solicitors fees would actually amount to:	£
1 The quote of £270, plus VAT of £47.25, making	317.25
2 Stamp Duty of 1% of the purchase price.	850.00
3 Other disbursements approximating	180.00
making a total of	1,347.25

£1,347.25 is approximately 16% of the buyer's available cash! This may go some way to explaining why solicitors have found it so difficult to increase their fees. The estate agent, of course, acts for the seller, who receives the money. Once a buyer has been found, the seller is eternally grateful for what the estate agent has done.

A fee of £270 does not sound unreasonable, but when the recession came solicitors were asking clients to ring them last and then quoting unprofitable prices. Unfortunately, those prices, created an awareness in the market place that all solicitors' fees, not only for conveyancing but for all work could be negotiated. Welcome to the market place from which solicitors had been protected for far too long.

What is the effect of this scenario on our conveyancer's view of the market place? She knows from her forecast not only that she wants to achieve £100,000 but that she needs to clear £67,000 just to break even. Unless she is going to work much longer hours (which is what is actually happening), she cannot charge less than £60 per hour (£67,000/1,125) to achieve break even. As has already been pointed out with the barrow boy, if she carries out the work out at less than £60 per hour (her break even figure) it doesn't matter how many conveyances she does within the 1,125 hours she has decided she needs to work, she will mathematically never recover her costs, never mind make a profit. If the average conveyance take three hours then her minimum fee to break even would be £180 (3 × £60).

If she increases her working day by one productive hour (or works on a Saturday for 5 hours), her annual working time would be approximately 1,350 (261 days less 33 for holidays, sickness and training = 228 + 1,125 = 1353). Her break even would then be £50 per hour (£67,000/1,350). This means that her minimum price to break even would be £150. There would of course be little point in her running her business on this basis as she would not be making money, unless by doing so she felt she could close down some of the competition. She might not be able to do that, but some larger institutions might think it was worthwhile!

How could she make money on this basis? The only way, other than working even longer hours, is to reduce her expenses. If she could get a licensed conveyancer to do the work and use computers to deal with all the paperwork, she may be able to achieve some saving. For example, the licensed conveyancer might settle for a wage of £25,000 per annum and a share of her typist, and the computerised system might increase capacity without increasing the cost significantly. Then she might be able to achieve a better profit with conveyancing at a cheaper level. She would have to find some other work to do, or she might decide merely to run the business and supervise the overall work.

The shape of the business might therefore look like this:

Her turnover might then be

Licensed conveyancer	80,000	
Her other fees	60,000	140,000

Her expenses might be

Wages say

Licensed conveyancer		25,000
Secretary		13,000
General office		10,000
Telephonist		10,000
		58,000

Expenses

Rent and rates	6,500		
Light and heat	1,600		
* Telephone	2,800		
* Postage	5,200		
* Stationery	2,000		
Books	800		
Insurance	1,200		
* Equipment leasing	3,750		
* Accountancy	1,500		
Indemnity Insurance	7,750		
Car	1,500		
* Bad debts	1,000		
Training CPD	700		
* Advertising	2,000	38,300	96,300
	Net profit		43,700

* Expenses increased by introduction of the licensed conveyancer

If you deduct her notional salary of say £25,000 her super profit will be £18,700. This represents approximately 13% of her new turnover, which is 5% better than it was and she is doing less work!

As the licensed conveyancer is expected to work 1,125 productive hours and has to achieve £80,000, his hourly charge-out rate will be approximately £70. If the average conveyance takes three hours, he need only charge £210 as against the solicitor's £270. This may be sufficient to give the solicitor the edge she requires.

It is not necessary to go down market to achieve the same result. If the solicitor decided to specialise, she might be able to increase her fees doing the same hours. The difficulty is, of course, that she needs to find a speciality which she can operate in her market place and is not in competition with other solicitors, who may be doing the same thing. On the present figures if she could increase her charge-out rate to £150 per hour, then on 1,125 she could make £168,750.

The calculation of time as suggested in this chapter does not take into account the artificial method required to calculate time to accommodate taxation. All clients have the right to insist on a remuneration certificate or a formal taxation if they are unhappy about the fee. In court and legally aided matters, specific time rules have to be observed. Clearly where the practice is regularly dealing with matters of that nature they must accommodate the necessary procedures. Whether they do or not will depend on the type of practice they are running. If the practice deals with predominantly non-contentious work, it would be nonsense to run the practice on the basis that every single bill is going to be taxed, or will require a remuneration certificate. It may be that the fee would be successfully agreed either on a taxation or a remuneration certificate in any event. As both exercises take an inordinate amount of time, and in the writers' experience do not arise very frequently, it would make commercial sense to accommodate the client if that is appropriate when such an occasion arises.

As has already been pointed out, time costing is an in-house calculation based on the assumptions of the partners as to what they could or should be earning. If they record the time accurately and charge their in-house rate, mathematically they will achieve the desired profit. The problem is that human nature is not like that. In the first instance time is not recorded accurately. Secondly, many partners and fee earners find it difficult to record more than five productive hours in a working day. This is perhaps because middle range solicitors typically handle in excess of 250 matters per year and tend to work on several at the same time. This can mean that it is not always possible to get a straight run at matters to record time effectively. Be that as it may, it is our belief that unless time can be recorded in a meaningful way the practice will suffer.

In working out the budget and forecast for the ensuing year, the partners must attempt to establish a shape that will produce the desired profit. It is therefore essential that they monitor the results. This means that the individual fee earner on his own or in the department must be accountable. He should maintain the agreed shape throughout the period. If he does not, he must be able to account for what has happened. If he has recorded his time correctly it will be possible to identify how he is spending his time and more particularly why he is not recovering all the time he is recording.

Quite frequently, practices will find that the amount of fees that can be recovered against the time recorded is discounted by about 20 to 25%. Under Rule 15 solicitors must advise their clients how they assess their charges and the likely cost. Supposing the partner's charge out rate is £200 per hour and he believes the work will take ten hours. He can advise the client that his cost will be £2,000. The client may or may not agree. Let us suppose that he does. The solicitor carries out the work but it takes longer than he thought, say 12 hours. This means he should charge £2,400. He feels, however, that the client would not agree to an increase, so he leaves the fee at £2,000. He renders his bill a little late – some two months after completion. By this time the client has forgotten how stressed he was when the work was being done and he rings the partner saying that he thinks the charge is a bit high. The partner's bills outstanding at the time may be higher than he would like them to be and he sees this bill as an opportunity to reduce the amount of his unpaid bills. He therefore agrees a discount to £1,800. This represents 75% of his actual time (£1800 × 100/£2,400).

If time has been recorded it is possible to ascertain on which particular matter the loss was made. This means that the partner will have to recover £400 (£2,400 – £1,800) somewhere else during the year if he is to achieve his figures. If he consistently under-charges then he will either have to undertake other work on which he can recover properly, or learn to be tougher with the clients. If, of course, the client will not pay any more the partner or fee earner must either work longer hours or find some other type of work.

> A solicitor rang his plumber late one night because the water tank in the attic was leaking. The plumber came, put it right and said "that will be £275". The solicitor said "You've only been here an hour, I'm a solicitor and I can't charge £275 per hour."
>
> "No" said the plumber, "Nor could I when I was a solicitor!"

The in-house figures identify the desired shape for the business, and time costing produces the in-house figures which enable the practice to charge at the desired rate. Later chapters will deal with how it is possible to ensure that the client pays at the right rate, either by persuading them to agree the costs or by organising the practice so that the fee charged is attractive in the market place and the work can be done at a profit. First, however, it is necessary to apply the ideas set out above to a typical practice by working out the budget and forecast.

How are you doing? Questions in relation to your practice and departments.

1. What are your gross fees?
2. What are the costs of:
   (a) wages;
   (b) other overheads?
3. What is net profit?
4. What are notional salaries?
5. What is the net profit percentage?
6. What is the super profit?
7. What is the super profit percentage?
8. What would the answers be if you related the super profit to the departments and are any of them breaking even or making a loss?
9. Is the shape of the whole practice satisfactory?

CHAPTER 2
FORECASTING AND BUDGETING

"If we are going to increase our share of profit we will need to increase the turnover by 5%."

"We'll increase the wages by the rate of inflation, but we can't increase our fees because the market is very competitive."

Both these propositions are commercially unacceptable, but it is surprising how many practices' partners start from these points of view.

Budgeting and forecasting can be a bit hit and miss in as much as partners are often unwilling to face the realities of their departments. Markets are always rising and falling; it depends where you perceive you are in the market as to the likely growth or otherwise in the various departments and consequently within the practice as a whole.

One thing is absolutely certain, however, whatever your budget or forecast is it will always be wrong. It is, after all, only a guestimate of what you feel might be achievable. If you check the actual results against the budget monthly and quarterly, it will be possible to see where things might be going wrong and do something about it. Quite frequently partners do not take any action when it is patently obvious that all is not well. There is a strong belief among the self-employed that it will be "all right on the night". Experience dictates differently.

In the last chapter it was suggested that all businesses have a shape and where possible an attempt should be made to try to achieve the optimum shape for a solicitors' office, that is 33% for wages, 33% for all the other expenses and 33% for the partners. This is a shape which is very difficult to achieve these days. An average of 25% is probably nearer the mark as a profit figure for the partners. This means that either the wages or other overheads exceed 33%. Usually it is the wages as, by and large, solicitors have been anxious to be fair to their staff even at their own expense.

The partners do not always appreciate that the only way to prepare a budget is from the bottom up. This means that you do not just add a percentage to last year's figures, but must examine every part of your office expenses in arriving at the likely budget and forecast for the current year. First you need to consider all the expenses to ensure that unnecessary expenditure is not being incurred. It is then necessary to look at what the individual partners and fee earners are actually doing by way of fees, to work out realistically what might properly be achievable.

The best place to start is with the figures from the previous year. In-house management figures ought to be available to give you a good starting point.

In this chapter and the next are tables showing all the sorts of figures that might typically be found in a medium sized practice. Messrs Bowles, Green & Howes, the mythical practice, have come a long way since 1976. They are now a ten-partner firm with 20 other fee earners, 28 secretaries, and a further 13 administrative staff. Their budget and forecast for their current year appears as Table 1. Their figures could be better but they need some serious strategic planning if they are to achieve the 33% shape. It is difficult to produce figures for a typical practice but these should not be a long way away from most middle sized practices. The same rules, however, apply to both large and small practices.

Rather than confuse you with a myriad of figures we propose to look at the typical types of expense that must be considered when building up the budget.

The full breakdown of the heads of the expenses is set out in Table 2. It is clear from these that the bulk of the overhead costs are fixed and that there is very little that can be done to make a meaningful reduction. If inflation is running between 2.3% and 2.8% then the expenses are likely to increase on a not dissimilar basis.

Like the Barrow boy it is essential that you identify your direct and indirect costs. The direct costs are those costs directly incurred by the fee earners and partners in earning the fees. These are costs, which need only be incurred if a fee earner, or partner is employed. The total of these costs, are deducted from the gross fees, the result expressed as a percentage of the turnover represents the gross profit margin.

DIRECT OVERHEAD COSTS

WAGES

The wages are those of the fee earners and secretaries who are involved in earning fees. The administrative wages are part of the indirect costs, which are incurred whilst the practice maintains its premises, and existing style of practice. From a commercial point of view staff can be employed and made redundant, as the work requires. Clearly there are financial consequences to such changes and they need to be considered carefully. In the budgetary function each department identifies the assistance they require and the level of wages. The problem is that each department tries to identify why their department needs assistance more than another. In the bigger practices even a modest wage rise across the board can be very expensive. The budget should be a time to address the proper level of wages so that you have the best staff for the purpose at the right wage. Staffing levels are a matter for the strategic meeting. Some practices continually put the wages up as "good employers" without actually working out how they are going to be paid. Perhaps even more common, the wages are discussed as the draft budget is being considered. The wage levels are fixed and it then transpires that the forecast of fees was not as high as was expected and the profit goes down. By that time the more enthusiastic partners have inadvertently told their staff what they are getting! Remember to include the appropriate rate of NIC. As will be seen later, computers have been integrated into many offices without any real consideration being given as to their added value. There is little point in installing computers if they are still being used as typewriters! It must be part of the rationale that the fee earners and partners use the computers so that the number of secretaries can be reduced. There is no good reason why fee earners and partners should not be able to produce some of their own documentation. This is particularly so where standard precedents are being used.

NOTIONAL SALARIES

Strictly speaking the notional salaries of the partners should be treated as a direct cost. Many of the comparisons prepared by outside organizations do not take notional salaries into account when considering the net margin. This is often on the basis that the net profit includes the notional salaries, because this represents the balance of the money due to the partners. This is misleading as it is certain that the partners could obtain employment elsewhere and when doing so, they would command a reasonable salary commensurate with their experience. As a result the net profit margin as identified in Table 1 show a percentage of 8% as against a net profit excluding the partners' notional salary of 24%. The considered view is that the net profit after deducting notional salaries should be nearer 15% than 8%.

TRAVEL AND ENTERTAINING

These represent expenses charged to the firm predominantly by members of staff for travel expenses and entertaining which cannot be charged specifically to a client.

TEMPORARY STAFF

This is an area which does bear some careful examination. It is, of course, a great ego trip to be so busy that extra staff are needed. But if such staff are carried as a central overhead then there is nothing to discourage a department from requisitioning such help. If temporary staff expenditure has to be bid for, then the department needs to identify why the expenditure is needed. It may well be that with a bit of careful planning other secretarial and typing members of the department could help out. This is invariably the result when the individual department has to pay for extra staff by way of temporaries out of their budget!

Temporary staff may be needed in the administrative department. The same considerations apply but the staff will be allocated to the indirect overhead costs discussed below.

OTHER DIRECT COSTS: TELEPHONES

The bulk of the calls will relate to business. If the business is expanding then clearly the cost will go up. It is, however, worth looking at your systems. There have been fundamental changes in the market place, which could significantly alter the cost of the service. Further it might make sense to separate the telephone and reception. The telephone can, after all, be manned from anywhere. It might make sense to monitor the use of mobile phones. A small amount of the expenditure could be private use by partners, fee earners, and members of staff. Clearly it is difficult to restrict telephone use. In fact it is arguable that restricting private calls altogether can be counter-productive. It would make more sense to allow such calls and rely on the integrity of the staff to honour the arrangement. After all if people are treated as adults then they tend to behave like adults.

OTHER DIRECT COSTS: PRINTING AND STATIONERY

This speaks for itself. Most practices have firms of printers that they use because, for example, they are clients. It might make sense from time to time to get a quote from another firm to be sure that you are getting best value.

OTHER DIRECT COSTS: POSTAGE AND SUNDRIES

Postage is fairly obvious save that it might be worth addressing the variations of first and second class and the DX arrangements. Sundries are a much more serious matter. This may be an area where some saving can be made. Quite frequently sundries are the depository for all those miscellaneous expenditures which cannot be identified to any specific heading. It is worth while checking what these consist of, as it might be found that there are items of expenditure which should be properly accounted for.

OTHER DIRECT COSTS: SUBSCRIPTIONS AND DONATIONS

These are the practicing certificates and membership of the various law societies and professional organisations.

OTHER DIRECT COSTS: EQUIPMENT LEASING AND RENTAL

These relate to those pieces of equipment which are necessary for the smooth running of the office. There is a lot to be said for the leasing of the more expensive pieces of equipment. This is for several reasons. Where the equipment is undergoing substantial updates on a fairly frequent basis it helps to lease because the equipment can be updated more easily than if it had been bought. The payment of rent appears as an expense and so long as the practice can maintain or increase its profit, the real cost goes down. However, if the practice gets into difficulties then the leasing of equipment can have serious repercussions. It makes sense to identify the equivalent capital value of the items from time to time. As the assets are being leased they do not appear on the balance sheet. It is sometimes a little disconcerting to realise the true cost of the asset. If a leasing contract is terminated there is usually a penalty. It is worth knowing what the potential liability might be if the worst happened and the practice had to dispose of the asset, usually when looking to replace it with another dealer. It is also useful to know what notional debt is building up as this might reach an unacceptable level. It might also reveal the true cost which in turn may persuade the practice to deal with these items on a different basis.

OTHER DIRECT COSTS: EQUIPMENT REPAIRS

These are usually covered by the suppliers of the principal pieces of equipment. There will, however, be pieces of equipment which are not covered by those maintenance contracts, which need repairing from time to time.

OTHER DIRECT COSTS: TRAINING

It is suggested later in the book that most practices will have to develop some kite marks such as Lexcel (the Law Society quality standard); ISO9001 and IIP to name three. In the future these may be the only way in which the clients (and particularly the larger corporate clients) will be able to select their solicitors. A direct result of such kite marks will be the need to train the individual staff within the disciplines the partners wish to promote. It would make sense then for the individual departments to identify how much they think they will need to cover their departments training needs. This will include the compulsory CPD hours. If the department has to "bid for" their share of that expense it will make them both careful and accountable for the expenditure. For example, is it really necessary for everyone to go on the same courses or would it be possible for the individual attending the course to address the department on the subject at a later date.

OTHER DIRECT COSTS: PRIVATE HEALTH

Many Practices fund private health care for all the staff and partners. If this benefit is in position it might be very difficult to withdraw it. If it is withdrawn the staff are likely to want an increase in their wages as compensation. There are all sorts of benefits in kind which need to be carefully consider as to their long term consequences. A one-off bonus payment might achieve the same effect without locking the practice into a continuing expense. This is a value judgment which only an individual practice can make for itself.

OTHER DIRECT COSTS: COST DRAFTING

Many practices have their own in-house cost-drafting department. This cost represents a direct overhead cost at least with regard to the litigation department. Much of it should be recoverable from the client.

DATA PROCESSING

Computers were going to solve all our problems; staff could be reduced, and profits would increase. It hasn't always worked out like that. This has a chapter on its own, however, it's well worth saying now that even the sophisticated users of computers have not actually worked out what saving, if any, has been produced to the bottom line. Fee earners and partners are possibly using them where they used secretaries before. This is because that is the only way with low priced routine work the margins can be maintained. It would be worth looking at the systems in place to assess whether you are getting value for money. Computers are changing so fast and the hardware is becoming so reliable that some maintenance contracts would bear looking at to see if they are needed. There is no doubt that if computers are bought on rental the expenditure can be the equivalent of several good secretaries. In the longer term it may well be worth employing a computer expert in-house. If a new fee earner is brought on board then they will need a computer, software, and a software license to work the system. The total of all the above are the marginal costs of running the office. Every time another fee earner is taken on or removed there is a direct increase or saving to the practice.

INDIRECT COSTS INCURRED IN MAINTAINING THE EXISTING BUSINESS

From what has been said so far it will be clear that there are some costs which you are stuck with whether you like it or not. These costs arise form the way in which the business has been run historically. If the practice has a town centre presence with two or three branch offices, then it is likely to maintain that shape unless the partners decide it is necessary to change the strategy. That will involve the partners in a lot of soul searching in a strategic meeting. Until such decisions are made the firm will incur these costs and can do very little about them. These costs are shared out between all the departments and represent the indirect overhead costs which each department has to earn before any profit at all can be made.

ADMINISTRATIVE WAGES

These are all the staff who are involved in the accounts department; telephone and reception and the general office. They will also include the office managers, IT co-ordinators, marketing and human resources. They are all the people who help the office to operate but do not make a direct contribution to the fees. The same considerations apply to them as to the other members of staff when considering their wages and position in the firm.

AUDIT AND ACCOUNTANCY

Although everyone should be paid on a proper basis it is amazing how easily solicitors accept that their professional colleagues should be paid properly, whilst agreeing discounts on their own fees at the drop of a hat! If your firm is not able to obtain an automatic 5% increase in fees, perhaps it would be worth asking the accountants why they should – assuming this is the case.

SOLICITOR'S INDEMNITY FUND

The profession has now got the opportunity of placing this liability in the market place. It is a sad comment on the times that we live in that the incidence of claims is growing. (Maybe the profession ought not to object too much, as a litigious environment helps to expand the litigation departments!) Frequently even the basic cover can represent 5% or more of turnover. Inevitably the firm has to cover a proportion of the overall risk themselves. It has been possible to cover that shortfall by paying an additional premium but the cost is nearly pound for pound of the savings. (If for example the firm has to find the first £80,000 of claims it is likely to cost £70,000 or more for the cover!) In those circumstances it might make sense to see what the average amounts of claims have been and where they lie. Armed with that information it might be possible to tighten up the procedures in the department giving rise to the most claims, and to save on a monthly basis sufficient amounts to cover the claims. Supposing the average claims have been £24,000 p.a., then it would make sense to set aside £2,000 per month to cover the liability. This could be set aside elsewhere than in the bank account. (For example in a Building Society.) Whether that amount is set aside in a separate account to meet the liability, or treated as a reserve to be deducted from the overdraft when considering the cash flow matters not, at least the money will stay with the practice, rather than be paid over to an insurance company as a premium.

It would be sensible to treat the amount as a reserve in the management accounts. There is also a lot of sense in looking at risk management. Risk management does, of course, have a soft cost which needs to be identified, but it should help to bring the incidents of claims down. Risk management is discussed in a later chapter.

ESTABLISHMENT COSTS

These represent rates, rent, light and heat, building maintenance; cleaning and security; and insurances. Depreciation is referred to below and the same considerations apply.

DEPRECIATION

This is not a cash figure and in a sense is not a true expense. However, it is inevitable that fixed assets and equipment essential to the running of the office will need to be replaced. Depreciation is in many ways an artificial figure, but it does not amount to a sinking fund to make the replacement possible. It merely creates an expense which recognises that at some stage money will have to be found to replace the asset. For tax purpose much of depreciation appears as capital allowances. The government from time to time gives special treatment to certain items. This can result in the allowance being 50% or more of the initial costs. Depreciation, on the other hand, is often worked out on a straight line basis over the useful life of the asset. Over a five year period for example this would amount to 20% of the value of the asset. It should be remembered that depreciation does *not* represent cash. It is a notional deduction from the profits (as an expense) so that due regard can be taken in the profits of the fact that items are being used and need replacing.

LIBRARY AND PUBLICATIONS

This is an area which can run away with expenditure because of lack of control. Clearly if each department has to identify the expenditure that they have in mind then there will be a much better control on the cost. It may also be that the department isn't using the text books it thought it was and indeed that some of the more routine texts can be found on the internet. Certainly where precedents are used, electronic publications which produce the precedents most usually used in the department could be better than books as there will be an automatic update of the text. These are discussed in more detail in a later chapter.

MARKETING AND ADVERTISING

The department will, as a result of working out its budget and forecast, be able to identify what it needs to do to promote itself. Marketing is discussed in more detail in a later chapter but would include general promotion of the department including advertising, articles, seminars, mail shots, databases etc and, where necessary, corporate or client entertainment. The practice will have to develop a business strategy for the medium and longer term and within the strategy will need to identify its priorities in relation to the marketing expenditure. It may therefore be that although a department would like to have an extensive spend on its marketing activity, the practice as a whole may wish to have a more comprehensive spend in a particular area of work. The need to bid for the items of expenditure will hopefully create a dynamic within the budgetary discipline, which not only identifies the level of expenditure but also creates accountability. The individual departments have to justify any over-spend and indeed show in the next budgetary round that they achieved what they hoped that they might achieve. If they do not then they will have to justify their requirements to their colleagues.

TRAVEL AND ENTERTAINING

This is a general expense not already catered for in the marketing and advertising budget. It represents expenditure within the practice for staff which cannot be identified anywhere else, nor charged to clients.

MOTOR EXPENSES

Firms have different ways of dealing with cars for partners and staff. In many cases the cars are leased. This enables the partners in some cases to have better quality cars. Quite frequently the lease contract also covers repairs and maintenance. Alternatively partners can be required to organise their own cars, although the practice might well agree to pay for the licensing insurance and maintenance together with a petrol allowance, as an extra drawing, debited to the appropriate partners in their capital accounts. Where cars are provide for staff it is necessary to bear in mind the tax provisions for benefits in kind. In some circumstances the staff might prefer a higher wage and to make their own arrangements. The benefit in kind provisions for staff and cars is far from satisfactory. If a reasonable mileage is being incurred it would probably make sense to increase the wages and stop contributing to the cost of the cars.

MANAGEMENT CHARGE

In simple terms this would be when a practice has a branch office which utilises the central administration of the principal office. This is principally the accounts and storage activities. As a result it is sensible to raise a charge to that office for the cost to the principal office if its true profitability is to be known.

BAD DEBTS

These represent the likely failure to recover bills outstanding in the twelve month period. The figure must be realistic otherwise profits and capital accounts are being unnecessarily inflated. There is, however, little point in deluding the partners as to the real worth of bills outstanding if they are unlikely to be paid. The reality will be that the partners will be taking cash out which is not replaced by the anticipated fees. Clearly the partners need to address fees unpaid properly by identifying the clients from whom they are due. If they have been outstanding for more than 12 months it is unlikely that they will be paid. There will be clients owing such money, which *will* be paid in a later period, but the partner or fee earner should be made to justify the amount of write off that they consider to be reasonable.

PROFESSIONAL FEES

Where a practice owns its property there should be a valuation taken at reasonable intervals to ensure that the balance sheet figure represents the correct value.

FINANCE COSTS

These represent the interest payable to the Bank, Building Societies, and other funders. Many firms have arrangement with their banks whereby the overdraft borrowing is set-off against the interest received on clients' account. The banks are a little more wary than they were ten years ago with the reduction in margins generally. Banks seem to agree different deals with different practices. If the client account is buoyant then no charges may be made for operating the account. A set-off of the overdraft interest against interest earned on client account and not defrayed to clients, should be possible. Set-off arrangements often hide the real cost of the borrowing, because the interest charge is not clearly identified. If the client balances fall for any reason, then the practice can find itself actually paying interest. The Bank will insist on a higher level of client account on which no interest is earned to set-off the interest which would otherwise be charged on the overdraft. It is important to make sure (on a regular basis) that the arrangements with the Bank are still the same as those originally negotiated.

FEES

It is a great deal easier to budget the expenses than forecast the fees. The starting point is not, however, adding 3 or 5% on to last year's figures. It is possible to be a great deal more sophisticated than that. Most offices now run their accounting systems on computer. Most computer packages produce a detail of the bills delivered by subject matter. In a probate department for example, you might find that the probate partner divided his work as 60% for probate, 20% for trusts and the balance on more miscellaneous work such as wills and small family matters, deeds of variation, powers of attorneys, etc. From available information the partners or fee earners can make a list of work done in the previous year, together with the fees earned in each area. They should also be able to identify the actual clients who are serviced by them. If all the departments have a fairly good idea of the type of work they have handled in the previous year, it ought to be possible to make an intelligent estimate of the likely fees for the current year.

A good number of last year's clients or those who refer business may be the same for the current year. Even if they are not, the partner or fee earner will have a good idea of the shape of their departments. They ought also to be able to see where the difficulties might be and make a real effort to try to attract new clients to fill the gaps.

Preparing a list in this way does three things:

1. It identifies the important clients you need to look after.
2. It makes you think whether you could cross-sell to some of the other departments to increase the work you can provide from these clients.
3. It makes you address where the rest of your fees are going to come from and what you need to do to bring new work into the practice.

When the partner and fee earners have all prepared what they believe to be reasonable figures, they can be assembled into departmental budgets and forecasts and then extrapolated into the overall budget and forecast for the practice. It might be necessary for each fee earner and partner to work out his or their best possible forecast and their worst. They could then take an average as their most likely achievable. However the budget and forecast is worked out, it needs to be realistic and achievable.

Once the budget and forecast have been agreed, it is necessary to ensure that the actual results are compared regularly with the budget and forecast to see where they differ if at all. Far too often monthly figures are ignored and partners and fee earners are not held accountable. It seems a nonsense not to look at the figures and make the necessary adjustments arising from them.

If the partners and fee earners have built up their budgets as identified in this chapter, they will probably own the figures and therefore be more readily accountable. Further they will be able to explain any discrepancies.

As has been mentioned earlier, margins appear to be under pressure. In the bigger practices this is undoubtedly because of the pressure on wages. The Americans have entered the City of London and have been offering wages at a much more substantial basis than have been available in the past. The only way these can be paid is to require the solicitors and fee earners to work longer hours. It is commonplace to be asked to work for 1,400 to 1,600 productive hours. Whether they can be maintained remains to be seen. Health and family constraints may make this impracticable in the long term. City practices might not only find that they are unable to keep quality staff for very long, but the resultant stress could produce a larger bill in compensation than the extra work generated. There needs to be a balance. This subject is discussed in more detail in Chapter 6.

CASH FLOW FORECAST

Once the forecast and budget are prepared it is necessary to prepare a cash flow forecast to assess what the effect of the forecast might be on the bank balance or overdraft. The timing of cash receipts seldom follows the budget, and quite frequently budgets and forecast have to be re-addressed when it is discovered that they have a negative effect both on the cash and the balance sheet. The next chapter deals with the compiling of a cash flow forecast.

All these principles have been applied to the practice of Messers Bowles Green & Howes. Analysis of Table 1 reveals:

- wages including the administrative staff in the previous year equal £879,835
- the other expenses for the previous year amount to £613,254

The wages represent 45% of the total turnover and the other overhead costs represent 31%. It will be recalled that the ideal shape would be 33% and 33%, leaving a profit of 33%.

- The net profit last year was 25% of turnover at £470,006
- Table 1 also identifies the wages for the current budget at £915,038

This represents 44% of turnover (£915,038 × 100/2,061,250)

If the ideal is 33%, then the 11% overspend represents £228,760 (£915,038 − [915,038 × 33/44] = £228,760.)

If the average secretarial wage is £14,000 to £16,000, this represents 14 to 16 members of staff. The practice is not going to be able to shed that number of staff. The improvement of "voice" for computers will undoubtedly alter the way partners and fee earners carry out their work. This, coupled with dedicated computer programs, ought to make it possible to have more than one

Table 1 Bowles, Green & Howes office budget 2000/2001

	1999/2000		2000/2001 Principal office		Branch office		Total
Fees	1,963,095		1,496,250		565,000		2,061,250
Wages/Consultancy							
Partners' notional salaries	35,000						
Fee earners and NI	315,000		245,000		70,000		315,000
Secretarial and NI	392,619		291,020		125,746		416,766
Direct overhead costs other	327,316		270,832		62,350		333,182
	291,691		214,380		89,700		304,080
Total Direct costs	**1,326,626**	68%	**1,021,232**	62%	**347,796**	66%	**1,369,028**
Admin and NI	159,900		113,090		54,900		167,990
Other	321,563		239,890		97,050		336,940
Total overhead expenses	**481,463**	25%	**352,980**	27%	**151,950**	24%	**504,930**
Total costs	**1,808,089**	92%	**1,374,212**	88%	**499,746**	91%	**1,873,958**
Net profit (loss)	**155,006**	8%	**122,038**	12%	**65,254**	9%	**187,292**
Partners' notional salaries	35,000		245,000		70,000		315,000
Profit before partners salaries	**470,006**		**367,038**		**135,254**		**502,292**
Percentage	24%		25%		24%		24%
Staff numbers							
Fee earners	19		12		8		20
Partners	10		7		3		10
Secretarial	27		23		5		28
Admin shared on basis of staff	13		9		4		13

fee earner to a secretary. As mentioned above, however, there is a trade off in that the cost of the computers goes up. They should not go up at the same rate as the wages do, but go up once and then remain static at least until more computers are needed. A saving of five secretaries would on the above figures put £80,000 on the bottom line (£16,000 × 5).

It will be clear when working through the expenditure that there isn't much room for manoeuvre. It is important to keep a careful eye on expenses, but it can be seen that no great savings can be made from the previous year if the business is going to keep the same sort of shape. It will be seen from Table 1 that the forecast of the rest of the expenses represent 31% of turnover, so the practice is within the range which it is trying to achieve.

A much more robust case can be made out when considering the fees and the time needed by each fee earner and partner to make them.

It will be seen from the table below that Mr Howes hopes to achieve fees of £130,000. These are made up as follows:

E Howes Commercial Department

Agro Chemicals PLC	25,000
Froom PLC	22,000
Prospect Properties Limited	18,000
Smith & Co	16,000
Leeland Ltd	9,500
Smithson's College	7,000
Brown's School	6,000
Louisa Trust	1,200
Martin trust	2,400
Charitable Trusts	3,500
Balance	19,400
Total	130,000

In this context Mr Howes must achieve a further £19,400 from other than his existing clients. If his average fee is £850 then he will need to take on 23 more clients (£19,400/£850 = 22.82). As this represents only two new instructions approximately each month it ought not to be too difficult to achieve.

Alternatively, if he works 1,000 productive hours a year, he will need to make £130 per hour (his charge out rate to achieve his target). Whether he can or not is a matter for him, but at least he will planning to do so at the start of the year – rather than halfway through the year, when he discovers that he is not achieving his target because he hadn't carried out the exercise at the beginning of the year.

BUSINESS MANAGEMENT FOR SOLICITORS

Table 2 Bowles, Green & Howes expenses for 2000/2001

Expenses	Principal office	Branch office	Total
Direct costs			
Travel and entertaining	6,500	2,100	8,600
Temporary staff	10,300	5,000	15,300
Telephones	23,000	12,000	35,000
Printing and stationery	38,000	6,500	44,500
Postages and sundries	31,000	9,750	40,750
Subscriptions and donations	18,000	7,500	25,500
Equipment leasing and rental	4,750	3,750	8,500
Equipment repairs	4,500	2,750	7,250
Training	18,300	11,400	29,730
Private health	20,000	5,750	25,750
Data processing costs			
Hard/software support	18,000	9,200	27,200
Equipment leasing	22,000	14,000	36,000
Total	**214,380**	**89,700**	**304,080**
Indirect costs			
Audit and accountancy	4,500	1,500	6,000
Solicitors indemnity fund	68,000	18,750	86,750
Establishment costs			
Rent and rates	22,500	9,850	32,350
Light and heat	4,000	2,000	6,000
Depreciation	26,000	12,100	38,100
Library and publications	15,540	3,900	19,440
Advertising and marketing	27,650	11,300	38,950
Motor expenses	2,700	500	3,200
Management charge	−15,000	15,000	0
Bad debts	28,000	12,000	40,000
Compensation claims	6,000	1,500	7,500
Professional fees	2,500	0	2,500
Building maintenance	4,000	5,000	9,000
Cleaning and security	12,000	6,000	18,000
Insurances	8,500	1,750	10,250
Finance cost			
Bank interest	6,000	400	6,400
Loan interest	12,000	7,000	19,000
Mortgage interest	28,000	0	28,000
Interest received	−23,000	−11,500	−34,500
Total indirect overheads	**239,890**	**97,050**	**336,940**
Total overhead costs	454,270	186,750	641,020

Table 3 Bowles, Green & Howes departmental budget 2000/2001 (Principal office)

	Litigation 40%	Conveyancing 12%	Family 16%	Commercial 17%	Private client 10%	Financial services 5%	Total
Fees	**595,000**	**185,000**	**245,000**	**255,000**	**145,000**	**71,250**	**1,496,250**
Direct costs							
Partners' Notional Salary	70,000	35,000	70,000	35,000	35,000		245,000
Fee earners and NI	119,720	29,500	48,200	41,600	26,000	26,000	291,020
Secretarial and NI	128,150	39,398	27,034	38,000	25,125	13,125	270,832
Direct overhead costs	86,773	30,626	40,834	25,521	20,417	10,290	214,380
Total direct costs	**404,643**	**134,524**	**186,068**	**140,121**	**106,542**	**49,334**	**1,021,232**
Indirect costs							
Admin and NI	45,864	17,885	21,614	11,643	10,680	5,404	113,090
Other	97,098	34,270	45,693	28,558	22,847	11,423	239,890
Total indirect costs	**142,962**	**52,155**	**67,307**	**40,201**	**33,527**	**16,827**	**352,980**
Net profit/(Loss)	**47,395**	**−1,679**	**−8,375**	**74,678**	**4,931**	**5,089**	**122,038**
Net profit Percentage of Fees	8%	−1%	−4%	29%	3%	7%	8%
Staff Numbers							
Fee Earners	5	2	2	1	1	1	12
Partners	2	1	2	1	1	0	7
Secretarial	10	3	4	3	2	1	23
Admin shared on basis of staff	3.65	1.28	1.72	1.07	0.85	0.43	9

Table 4 Bowles, Green & Howes breakdown for the commercial department budget 2000/2001

	Fees	Fee Earner Annual	NI	Total	Fee Earner	Secret-aries Wage	NI	Total	Training Marketing Library	Over-head Admin	Total Expenses	Profit	%	Notional Salary	Net Profit	%
Fee earner																
Partner																
E Howes	130,000	0			J Jones	12,240	1,224	13,464	6,222	35,299	54,985	75,015	58.00	35,000	40,015	31
A Smith	80,000	25,320	2,532	27,852	M Donald	12,240	1,224	13,464	3,773	21,724	66,813	13,187	17.00	0	13,667	17
Trainee	45,000	12,499	1,249	13,748	V Barnes	10,066	1,006	11,072	2,505	12,219	39,544	5,456	14.00	0	6,108	14
Totals	255,000	37,819	3,781	41,600		34,546	3,454	38,000	12,500	69,242	161,342	93,658	38.00	35,000	60,658	24

Table 5 Bowles, Green & Howes administration budget 2000/2001 (Principal office)

	Basic month	Annual	NI Band	NI	Total
Admin					
Practice manager	1,825	21,900	10%	2,190	24,090
Cashier	1,026	12,310	10%	1,230	13,540
Assistant cashier	958	11,496	10%	1,149	12,645
Assistant cashier	958	11,496	10%	1,149	12,645
Clerk	817	9,804	10%	980	10,784
Telephonist	850	10,200	10%	1,020	11,220
Telephonist	807	9,684	10%	968	10,652
General office	695	8,340	5%	417	8,757
General office	695	8,340	5%	417	8,757
	8631	103570	0.8	9520	113090

Table 4 reveals the individual contributions to the profit by each of the fee earners in the department. If Mr Howes achieves his target of £130,000 he will contribute £40,015 to bottom line. It should be noted that a notional salary has been deducted from his profits on the basis that he could earn this elsewhere. Even so a contribution of 31% is clearly very satisfactory.

It will be noted that he thinks he will need to spend £6,222 on his training, books and library. His share of the overheads is £35,299 which is calculated as a proportion of his fees to the total overhead for the department. These figures include the salaries for the fee earners, trainee, and secretarial staff. When fixing the salaries remember the NIC liability. These have been fixed at 10% and will of course represent a monthly cash outlay. Quite frequently when fixing salaries NIC is forgotten.

Mr Howes and his fee earners have to identify the amounts they believe they will require for temporaries, training, books and marketing. If during the year they exceed these figures, they will have to justify the over-expenditure to the other partners. If they do not need as much then they will need to justify their expenditure in these areas for the following year.

The forecast for the anticipated fees appears in the first column, giving a total for the department of £255,000. This represents additional contributions from Mr Smith, a solicitor (£80,000) and the Trainee (£45,000). It might well be that both Mr Smith and the Trainee also help Mr Howes with some of his own work, for which Mr Howes gets the credit. The department budget reveals the relative contributions from the fee earners.

The figure for super profit is arrived at by deducting a notional salary of £35,000 from the fees of each of the partners. The Law Society proposes a figure of £31,500 for the provinces and £41,450 for London for the year 2000/2001. It is arguable, however, that the figure should represent the sort of income a Partner of Mr Howes' stature might achieve in the open market. If the profit does no more than pay the salary he might get elsewhere, there would seem little point in carrying on in practice. The practice under discussion is paying one of their assistant solicitors £35,000 and it is for that reason that the notional salary has been pitched at £35,000.

Applying the principles which applied to the barrow boy it is clear that it costs the firm £54,117 to have Mr Howes in the office. If he succeeds in recording 1,000 hours per annum, he will have to charge his time out at least £54 per hour (£54,117/1000 = £54.12) merely to cover those expenses. If he charges less than £54 per hour, he will not cover those costs never mind make any profit. His break even is therefore £54 per hour. If he wants to achieve his target, then he must charge £130 per hour (£130 × 1000 = £130,000). Whether he can or not will depend on the market place. As a result it is imperative that he and the practice keep a check on how things are going.

Each month his fees will be known. He needs to bill on average £10,833 per month. If he consistently fails to achieve that, the practice needs to know why and he needs to indicate what he proposes to do about it.

Mathematically, of course, it makes sense to increase the productive hours. If Mr Howes worked 1,400 productive hours, his hourly rate would become £81.25 (£130,000/1,600 = £81.25). In an already competitive market this would clearly mean that he could achieve the same fees at a much more attractive rate. This in turn may encourage clients to come to him because he is cheaper. He will not make any more profit: this will remain the same. The better answer, as indicated earlier in the book, is for him to employ a paralegal who can charge £81 per hour at half his costs and for Mr. Howes to find more complex or specialised work that he can charge at a much higher level.

The overall budget and forecast, as it might appear when all the partners and fee earners have had their say, appears in Table 1. From these figures the partnership should achieve approximately 24% as its net profit. The Commercial Department appears the most profitable producing a contribution of 38%. When corporate property and commercial business generally are buoyant there is no doubt that those practices concentrating on commercial work will be able not only to command higher fees but also, inevitably, to take home much larger profits.

Table 3 shows that deducting a notional salary as a direct cost and thereby reflecting the true cost of the department makes things not quite as rosy. The conveyancing department is making a loss of 1% and the family department is making a loss of 4%. This underlines the proposition that the more paralegals that can be used the better the margins. If this is coupled with a reduction in secretarial staff, the margins may improve substantially. It also underlines the proposition that partners should not be doing routine work at pedestrian fees. There are several practices around who have, as a result of this sort of analysis, parted company with some of their partners. It is not surprising, therefore, that there is a disincentive amongst some partners to become involved with the budgetary exercise!

Whatever way the budget and forecast comes out it will be necessary to see what the cash consequences might be. Those consequences may require the budget and forecast to be revisited. The cash flow forecast is dealt with in the next chapter.

How are you doing? Questions in relation to your practice and departments.

1. What percentage of turnover are your wages? Is this acceptable, and if it is not is there anything you can do about it?
2. What percentage of turnover are your fixed costs? Is this acceptable and if it is not is there anything you can do about it?
3. Have you prepared your forecast in relation to the fees you did last year with an estimate of what might be achievable this year?
4. Has the rest of the office prepared their forecasts on the same basis?
5. Is your own and the office's super-profit margin better than 15%?
6. If not, is there anything you can do to ensure that at least 15% can be achieved?
7. Have you prepared your budget from the bottom up?

CHAPTER 3
CASH FLOW

"At last! We have just collected two large bills of over £40,000; perhaps the partners could have a drawing!"

In the 1970s very few solicitors had overdrafts. This was principally because they had low overheads, few clients objected to their bills and competition was not particularly fierce. How things have changed! Not only are overdrafts very common but they are frequently used as a means of providing the capital needs of the practices.

What has happened in some cases is that partners have bolstered their income by securing an overdraft based on their anticipated work in progress and their outstanding bills and disbursements. This has effectively made more cash available, so in some cases they have been able to sustain their drawings at a higher level than the cash coming in might allow. With the reduction of work in conveyancing for the provincial practices and the increase in litigation work (which can take a long time to be paid) the banks have started to be less enthusiastic about the funding arrangements.

It is essential that partners should understand that the bills delivered do not necessarily represent the same amount of cash receipts. Further, there are payments made out of the practice on a cash basis which are not immediately obvious from the profit and loss account. It is therefore imperative that the practice prepares a "cash flow forecast".

The principles are the same as preparing the budget and forecast, but relate solely to the cash received and spent.

The purpose of preparing a budget and forecast is to anticipate the likely requirements of the practice to match the desired profit. Unfortunately profit is not cash, but without the latter, however profitable the firm may be, serious problems can arise.

For example, the litigation department may have decided to offer a "no win, no fee" service to the clients. From a purely legal point of view this makes eminent sense because everybody is doing it – and you have to compete. The concept does, however, require careful consideration of the cash implications. Supposing the practice anticipates handling 1,200 matters on this basis. It is clear that where possible only likely winners should be taken on. Insurances of various types can be obtained to underwrite potential costs, but there are bound to be some costs which the firm will have to take on. Clearly there will be court fees together with basic expert advice. Most experts will be asked to wait for payment, as the solicitor has to do, but even so an expenditure of £320 per case is probably likely. If the average case is going to take say nine months from start to finish then three-quarters of the 1,200 cases must be paid for before any money starts coming in. This amounts to 900 cases at £320 or £288,000 over the period. Interest at say 2% over base would add a further £18,000 to £20,000. Neither of these figures is an inconsiderable sum. If the cash consequences are not worked out on a forecast model before the decision is taken, the practice might find itself running out of money.

All forecasts are attempts to anticipate the consequences of business decisions so that there are no surprises later; and that is true of a cash forecast. However, the cash forecast is the consequence of the budget and forecast, so that if it shows a negative result it will be necessary to go back to the drawing board and reconsider the earlier forecasts.

FEES

The starting point for the cash forecast is the fees of the practice. The fees represent the forecast bills suggested by all the fee earners and partners. They do not represent the anticipated cash, however, for several reasons.

- The forecast fees represent the bills to be delivered during the current year.

- The practice will be receiving fees that are due from an earlier period but which are only now being paid.

- It is therefore necessary to know what the time lag on the bills might be.

- All the computer systems for accounts identify not only the total of the bills and disbursements outstanding, but also break them down into the individual fee earners and partners and by the number of months outstanding. It is therefore possible to identify where the problems are.

- The average time to pay is calculated by first dividing last year's turnover (excluding interest and commission) by 365 days. The resulting figure gives the average amount of money billed each day. If you then divide the bills outstanding figure by the average money billed each day, you will be able to say how many days those bills represent. The 2000 report by PriceWaterhouseCoopers on solicitors' practices surprisingly reveals that bills outstanding are in excess of 100 days and in some practices considerably more.

- If 100 days is 27% of the year then the bills outstanding will be 27% of the turnover.
- In arriving at this year's likely cash receipts, it would be sensible to discount the forecast by 27%.
- The fees from an earlier period will be being paid in addition to 73% of the forecast (100% − 27%).
- If the practice is growing, the higher fees thus generated will take some time to take effect. If the firm is slimming down, the balance may well be the other way. Either way it is certainly worth knowing.

If the fees for the year are £2,000,000, the cash receipts will be 73% of that figure (£1,460,000). If the bills outstanding from the previous year were calculated on the same basis then, if the turnover was £1,700,000, 27% of the bills outstanding would be £459,000 (£1,700,000 × 27%).

On an annual basis this represents a total cash receipt before VAT of:

- £1,460,000 + £459,000 = £1,919,000.
- If VAT is added to this figure the total becomes £2,254,825.
- On the face of it a turnover of £2,000,000 would attract VAT of £350,000, making a total of £2,350,000.
- If you take 95% of that figure (i.e. a reduction of 5%), you get £2,232,500 which is not a long way from the figure of £2,254,825.

Hence the suggestion that the total turnover plus VAT be reduced by 5%. It is as well to be conservative in any event. The figures can always be amended if they come out higher on a regular basis as the year progresses.

If fees are falling, a larger discount might be prudent. What is more, the bills outstanding figure does not necessarily represent all that will be paid in the next 3 months, and it is prudent to average them over 12 months.

Some inspired guesswork is required. Table 6 suggests a discount of 5%. As the year develops and the figures can be compared with the forecast you will get to know if you got it right. Either way, having the model to work to at least enables you to know why you get it right or wrong!

Table 6 Bowles, Green & Howes discount for 2000/2001

		VAT	Total	Discount
Principal office				5%
Litigation	595,000	104,125	699,125	664,169
Conveyancing	185,000	32,375	217,375	206,506
Family	245,000	42,875	287,875	273,481
Commercial	255,000	44,625	299,625	284,644
Private client	145,000	25,375	170,375	161,856
Finacial services	71,250	12,468	83,718	79,532
Branch Office				
Litigation	198,600	34,755	233,355	221,687
Conveyancing	65,000	11,375	76,375	72,556
Family	152,400	26,670	179,070	170,117
Commercial	85,000	14,875	99,875	94,881
Private client	64,000	11,200	75,200	71,440
Total	2,061,250	360,718	2,421,968	2,300,870

VAT

VAT has not been discussed up to now because it does not represent a profit for the partners. It might account for some interest earned, or overdraft interest saved, from the three months accumulation of the liability.

- VAT will be chargeable on all fees which are not otherwise zero-rated or exempt. The most likely source of exempt fees will arise in those practices giving advice in financial services. As a result the bulk of all fees delivered will be plus VAT at 17.5%.

- VAT will be paid out on the quarterly cycle based on the VAT charged in the fees less any VAT recoverable on payments made by the practice that are subject to VAT.

- VAT will be received as and when a fee is paid but, for VAT accounting purposes, in the appropriate quarter it is treated as having been received when the bill is sent out, whether it is paid or not.

As mentioned above, in preparing the forecast of cash receipts it is necessary to calculate the likely amount of VAT received. This will include the VAT on the older bills now being paid. It is difficult to be precise as to the amount that should be allowed.

VAT will be discussed in more detail in Chapter 4.

Table 7 Bowles, Green & Howes projected and actual fees to 30 April 2001

	May	Jun	Jul	Aug	Sept	Oct	Nov	Dec	Jan	Feb	Mar	Apr	Total
Principal office													
Litigation	37,907	52,189	37,907	44,569	44,569	44,569	61,328	62,770	53,530	49,521	49,521	56,620	595,000
Conveyancing	11,778	20,051	11,778	13,858	13,858	18,305	14,627	14,627	14,627	15,397	19,844	16,250	185,000
Family	15,599	21,488	15,599	18,352	18,352	24,240	19,372	19,372	24,724	20,391	23,603	23,908	245,000
Commercial	16,236	16,236	16,236	19,100	31,589	19,100	20,162	32,192	20,162	21,223	21,223	21,541	255,000
Private client	9,232	16,203	9,232	10,861	17,841	10,861	11,465	11464	11,457	12,067	12,067	12,250	145,000
Financial services	4,536	4,536	7,966	5,336	5,336	5,336	5,633	9,060	5634	5,929	5,930	6,018	71,250
Branch office													
Litigation	12,610	12,611	12,611	14,876	19,675	14,876	15,702	20,501	20,502	16,529	18,930	18,930	198,353
Conveyancing	4,869	5,713	4,138	4,869	4,868	6,443	5,139	6,714	5,139	5,394	5,394	6,969	65,649
Family	9,702	13,367	9,703	11,416	11,416	11,416	12,050	15,713	15,713	12,684	16,347	12,653	152,180
Commercial	5,409	5,409	5,409	10,460	6,367	6,367	10,814	6,720	6,720	7,074	7,074	7,074	84,897
Private client	4,075	4,075	6,588	4,794	4,794	4,794	5,061	5060	5,060	7,146	6,236	6,238	63,921
Total	131,953	171,878	137,167	158,491	178,665	166,307	181,353	204,193	183,268	173,355	186,169	188,451	2,061,250

Note: For cash flow add VAT of 17½% and take 95% of that figure in each month.

PROJECTED CASH RECEIPTS

Once you have identified the likely annual fees for each department (and where necessary added them to the other fees from other branches), it is necessary to extrapolate the results by month to obtain a likely shape for the receipts over the year. It is arguable whether an attempt should be made to guess the likely receipts in each department for each month or whether a straight line could be used. This depends to a certain extent on the size of the practice and the specialities within it. In a reasonably sized practice with an average spread of business, it is probably satisfactory to use a straight line.

It would be prudent to build the fees up over the 12-month period so that the anticipated forecast for the first six months will be less than those for the last six months. If, however, there are some parts of the office which have recognisable seasonal variation it might be important to know where the highs and lows of the likely cash receipts may be.

For example (see Table 6), in an office with a large probate department it might be prudent to recognise that a large proportion of the fees may fall some 12 months after the death. As more deaths occur around the winter and spring than in the middle of the year, this means that the largest fees may well fall in February, March and April for instructions received in the previous year.

Similarly fees in a litigation department, certainly where personal injuries are concerned, tend to be received in the second half of the year. Whether this is because people need the money around Christmas or most insurance companies' year ends are in December is unclear. If this is the way the department behaves then it would be foolish to forecast the fees at their best in May or June!

Having decided if there is a need to take account of seasonal variations, it is possible to make an intelligent guess of the likely cash receipts including VAT, with a suitable discount, which might be achieved from the forecast of fees for the current year. These figures will appear at the top of the forecast as monthly receipts for the year in question.

EXPENSES

Having established the likely receipts of cash for the year, broken down and discounted for each month, it is necessary to deduct the expenses. This is a much easier exercise because the budget will have set the level of expenses for the year and these were always going to be cash out-goings. It probably makes sense to extrapolate these into the cash flow forecast in a straight line as the figures will even themselves out over the year (see Table 8). There are areas where there will be seasonal adjustments. For example the Christmas bonus; the use of temporaries during the holiday period; the payment to the accountants; and bank interest paid quarterly on any funding which has not been secured by way of set off.

The figures can be included in full in the forecast but it is simpler to work them out on a separate sheet and merely carry the bottom line totals for each month to the cash forecast. This makes the forecast easier to follow as it is effectively not cluttered by all the expenses.

BANK INTEREST

The arrangements with the banks for individual practices seem to be legion. Some of the most common are as follows.

SET OFF

If the client account is receiving interest, the bank will agree that any overdraft interest can be set off against some of the interest that would otherwise be paid to the practice. The bank will insist that the amount of moneys held for clients to be used in the set off arrangement should be cleared funds and it will be a matter of negotiation. It would be helpful to look at the client account to see what the cleared funds have been. So for example if a facility of £250,000 is going to be needed for no win no fee work, then the bank might agree an overdraft of £250,000 with no interest charge, secured against cleared funds of say £300,000. It is only possible to make these arrangements, of course, if the client account is healthy.

It would be prudent not to have too much in a set off arrangement in case the market place changes dramatically so that the amount of clients' money falls, or interest can no longer be kept by the practice. The interest charge in those circumstances would then become a cash payment due from the practice.

INTEREST ON CLIENT ACCOUNT

A practice of the size and type of work of Bowles, Green and Howes may have a client account of £2,500,000 to £3,000,000. It is important to remember that clients are entitled to interest on money held by the practice at such reasonable market rate as the practice can achieve. If some moneys are invested with buildings societies at say 4%, that rate would have to be paid to the client. With large

Table 8 Bowles, Green & Howes projected and actual expenses to 30 April 2001

	Forecast	May	Jun	Jul	Aug	Sept	Oct	Nov	Dec	Jan	Feb	Mar	Apr	Total
Wages	915,038	75,744	75,744	75,744	75,744	75,744	75,744	75,754	81,844	75,744	75,744	75,744	75,744	915,038
Bonus	2,900			2,900										2,900
Direct costs														
Travel and entertaining	8,600	717	717	717	717	717	717	717	717	717	717	717	713	8,600
Training	29,730	2,477	2,477	2,477	2,477	2,477	2,477	2,477	2,477	2,477	2,477	2,477	2,483	29,730
Temporary staff	15,300			5,100	5,100						5,100			15,300
Telephones	35,000	1,916	2,916	3,916	1,916	2,916	3,916	1,916	2,916	3,916	1,916	2,916	3,924	35,000
Printing and stationery	44,500	3,708	3,708	3,708	3,708	3,708	3,708	3,708	3,708	3,708	3,708	3,708	3,712	44,500
Postages and sundries	40,750	3,396	3,396	3,396	3,396	3,396	3,396	3,396	3,396	3,396	3,396	3,396	3,394	40,750
Management charge	0													0
Private health	25,750	2,145	2,145	2,145	2,145	2,145	2,145	2,145	2,145	2,145	2,145	2,145	2,155	25,750
Subscriptions and donations	25,500	2,125	2,125	2,125	2,125	2,125	2,125	2,125	2,125	2,125	2,125	2,125	2,125	25,500
Equipment repairs	7,250	606	604	604	604	604	604	604	604	604	604	604	604	7,250
Equipment leasing and rental	8,500	712	708	708	708	708	708	708	708	708	708	708	708	8,500
Hard/software support	27,200	2,267	2,267	2,267	2,267	2,267	2,267	2,267	2,267	2,267	2,267	2,267	2,263	27,200
Equipment leasing	36,000	3,000	3,000	3,000	3,000	3,000	3,000	3,000	3,000	3,000	3,000	3,000	3,000	36,000
Indirect costs														
Motor expenses	3,200	267	267	267	267	267	267	267	267	267	267	263	267	3,200
Library and publications	19,440	1,620	1,620	1,620	1,620	1,620	1,620	1,620	1,620	1,620	1,620	1,620	1,620	19,440

Advertising and marketing	38,950	3,244	3,246	3,246	3,246	3,246	3,246	3,246	3,246	3,246	3,246	3,246	38,950
Solicitors indemnity fund	86,750	7,229	7,229	7,229	7,229	7,229	7,229	7,229	7,229	7,229	7,229	7,231	86,750
Audit and accountancy	6,000					6,000							6,000
Bad debts	40,000	3,333	3,333	3,333	3,333	3,333	3,333	3,333	3,333	3,333	3,333	3,337	40,000
Compensation claims	7,500	625	625	625	625	625	625	625	625	625	625	625	7,500
Professional fees	2,500			2,500									2,500
Rent and rates	32,350	2,735	4,135	2,635	2,635	4,135	2,535	2,635	4,135	2,635	2,635	1,500	32,350
Light and heat	6,000	500	500	500	500	500	500	500	500	500	500	500	6,000
Building maintenance	9,000	750	750	750	750	750	750	750	750	750	750	750	9,000
Cleaning and security	18,000	1,500	1,500	1,500	1,500	1,500	1,500	1,500	1,500	1,500	1,500	1,500	18,000
Insurances	10,250	856	854	854	854	854	854	854	854	854	854	854	10,250
Depreciation	38,100	3,170	3,170	3,170	3,170	3,170	3,170	3,170	3,170	3,170	3,170	3,170	38,040
Finance cost													
Bank interest	6,400		1,600			1,600			1,600			1,600	6,400
Loan interest	19,000	1,583	1,583	1,583	1,583	1,583	1,583	1,583	1,583	1,583	1,583	1,587	19,000
Mortgage interest	28,000	2,333	2,333	2,333	2,333	2,333	2,333	2,333	2,333	2,333	2,333	2,337	28,000
Total Expenses	1,593,458	128,558	132,552	138,452	136,052	132,552	136,352	128,462	138,652	130,452	133,552	129,913	127,849	1,593,398
Less interest received	34,500													
Total Costs	1,558,958													

Table 9 Bowles, Green & Howes projected cash flow to 30 April 2001

	May	Jun	Jul	Aug	Sept	Oct	Nov	Dec	Jan	Feb	Mar	Apr	Total
Discounted fees	147,293	191,859	153,112	176,916	199,434	185,640	202,434	227,931	204,573	193,507	207,812	210,359	2,300,870
Expenses less interest/deprec	122,508	126,508	132,408	130,008	126,508	130,308	122,418	132,608	124,408	127,508	123,863	121,805	1,520,858
Drawings	23,640	23,640	23,640	23,640	23,640	23,640	23,640	23,640	23,640	23,640	23,640	23,640	283,680
Income tax			70,355						70,355				140,710
Partners' motor expenses	3,962	3,962	3,962	3,962	3,962	3,962	3,962	3,962	3,962	3,962	3,962	3,962	47,544
VAT payment		62,008			64,572			67,813			69,875		264,268
Total payments	150,110	216,118	230,365	157,610	218,682	157,910	150,020	228,023	222,365	155,110	221,340	149,407	2,257,060
Difference fees/payments	−2,817	−24,259	−77,253	19,306	−19,248	27,730	52,414	−92	−17,792	38,397	−13,528	60,952	43,810
Opening balance	−244,726	−247,543	−271,802	−349,055	−329,749	−348,997	−321,227	−268,853	−268,945	−286,737	−248,340	−261,868	
Bank overdraft	−247,543	−271,802	−349,055	−329,749	−348,997	−321,267	−268,853	−268,945	−286,737	−248,340	−261,868	−200,916	

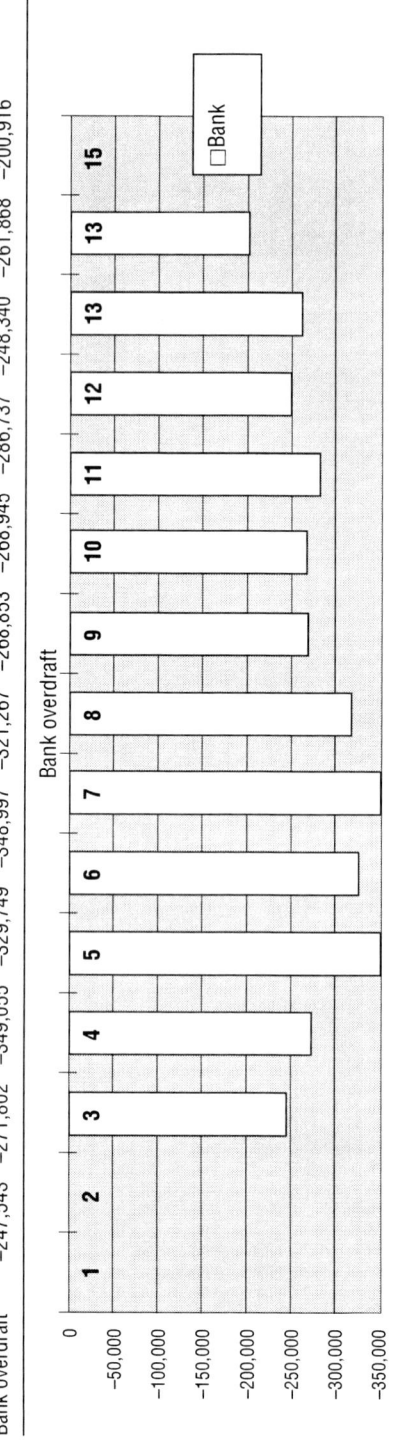

Bank overdraft

sums involved a practice can agree 1.5% to 2% over base rate as its overdraft rate and 1.5% to 2% under base rate as the credit for interest.

OPEN-ENDED FUNDING

The bank might allow an overdraft facility which only becomes repaid when the practice ceases to trade. This would be on the principle that there are a large number of partners coming and going, who can finance the facility without a requirement of repayment of the capital.

DEPRECIATION

It will be recalled that depreciation is not cash. It is merely an item of expenditure which recognises that capital items need to be replaced from time to time. It is therefore proper to deduct a notional figure from the profit to give credit for the ultimate expenditure, when the item has to be replaced. In an ideal world it would make sense to create a sinking fund into which the depreciation is actually paid, so that there would be an appropriate fund from which future items could be purchased. It does not however represent a cash payment and must be ignored when considering the figures to appear in the expenses in the cash flow forecast.

DRAWINGS

As you have prepared a forecast and budget then the anticipated profit will be known. It will also be possible to calculate the tax due from each partner. If the firm pays for the motoring expenses these will also be known. As a result it will be possible to calculate how much profit each partner hopes to achieve over the year. From that figure will be deducted his or her tax liability for the year, the car and any other expenses to arrive at the amount he or she could draw. As the forecasts and budgets are never right it would make sense to restrict the amount of drawings to perhaps 85% of that balance. This will allow for a little bit of slippage and will ensure that the partners do not over-draw.

CAPITAL ACCOUNTS

While the individual capital accounts do not impinge directly on cash flow, it would be prudent to mention them here. There are firms who have very large capital accounts for the partners, with a consequential small or no overdraft facility. Alternatively, there are firms with very large overdraft facilities and very low capital accounts. Neither is right although clearly large overdrafts do leave less room for manoeuvre if times get tough. However, large capital accounts can lead to increased overdrafts or further borrowings by partners if a senior man or woman leaves.

Many firms have a provision that where capital accounts are in credit (after say the first £2000 or £3000), interest is payable. After all, if the other partners had to borrow equivalent amounts to allow those partners to withdraw part of their excess on capital account an interest charge would arise. If, on the other hand, partners' capital accounts become overdrawn, interest would be chargeable to that partner until the account is back in balance. The problem with drawing up to the limit is that capital accounts can fluctuate wildly. Tax bills will vary particularly where pension provisions have been made.

Once a figure has been agreed as a drawing for the partners, the monthly payments can be calculated and appear in the forecast.

A balance has be struck with which the partners are happy. In past years drawings have not always kept up with cash receipts which has resulted in overdrafts increasing. It would be sensible to require the partners to put in a reasonable amount of capital from their own resources. They should have little difficulty in borrowing money from the bank on a fairly long-term basis if the business is successful. The balance of the funding can come from the overdraft. Again this must be fixed at a sustainable level. A down-turn in fees, or a poor year for other reasons could, if the facility is high, lead to unnecessary tensions. The consequence of a restriction on the overdraft, of course, is a restriction on drawings. It is for this reason that a middle ground should be found. The only problem with overdrafts is that sometimes they have to be repaid when it is least convenient to repay them!

If capital is to be introduced, that will be cash in the firm and will appear in the cash flow immediately below the anticipated fee income.

INCOME TAX

Prior to self-assessment, the income tax of the partners was a joint and several liability. Now individual partners are responsible for their own tax, although a partnership return is also required. Many practices have in the past saved the tax liability within their firms and they will have continued to do so, even though the liabilities are personal to each partner. It would make sense to save the tax for the partners as this prevents the more adventurous spending their tax liabilities as a drawing and then finding themselves in difficulties at the end of the tax year. It would be no consolation to the other partners that the liability was not theirs!

Income tax is payable in January and July each year. It will be a fairly high figure and appears under those months. Income tax is discussed in more detail in Chapter 4.

PARTNERS' MOTOR AND OTHER EXPENSES

Although these have been deducted for the purposes of establishing drawings, the drawing figures represents just the drawings and no more. It is necessary to account for the monthly cost of the cars and other expenditure in the cash forecast. These can be include on a straight line basis.

VAT PAYMENT

VAT is payable on a three-monthly cycle. The cycle can be different for each firm. The payment represents the VAT on the bills that have been delivered (whether paid or not) less any VAT paid on items of expenditure, that were subject to VAT. If the fees are likely to grow then the VAT will increase. The increase would however appear towards the end of the year.

TOTAL

Each column is then added up to give the total of the likely outgoings each month. The expenses are then deducted from the fee income giving a plus or minus figure each month. Armed with this information it is then possible to assess what the cash needs of the practice will be.

It is first necessary to add the monthly total to the bank balance at the end of the previous year (or subtract it from the balance as appropriate). This will appear in the balance sheet for the previous year. If the cash for the first month is positive and the firm is in overdraft, the positive figure is deducted from the overdraft. Conversely if the cash is negative the amount is added to the overdraft figure. This gives a bottom-line figure for the likely cash position at the end of that month. The new balance is carried forward to the next month and the same calculation is made. It will become immediately obvious that the cash is under its most severe pressure when VAT and tax have to be paid.

It is essential with all these forecasts that the partners make a contribution to their construction, understand how they are constructed, so that they own and take responsibility for them. They may then realise that the results require them to do something about the forecasts if things start to go wrong.

GRAPHS

Partners generally find it difficult to identify trends from a row of figures. All computers have graphing facilities, which will also identify the average position. If the graph or bar chart is produced with the figures then they will be more readily understood. A bar chart of the cash flow forecast for the fictitious practice used as the example in this book appears as Table 9.

BILLS OUTSTANDING AND DISBURSEMENTS

Most computer software these days will produce details of the bills and disbursements outstanding. These should be split between the various fee earners and departments. The balance sheet will show the amount due to the firm at the balance sheet date. Most practices like to think that they allow their clients 60 days to pay their accounts. The truth is that the bills are usually outstanding for longer than that. If you divide the turnover by 365 days that will give you the average amount of fees taken daily. If you divide that daily figure into the bills outstanding as shown on the balance sheet you will discover the average number of days bills outstanding. As mentioned above, the figure for the practice under discussion is 57 days. We would be surprised if many practices can achieve that.

Bills outstanding represent work done and there is no good reason why they should not be paid promptly. A client is unlikely to come back to you if his or her bill is outstanding. Even where you act for substantial organisations there should be an opportunity to suggest that work cannot be done unless the fees are brought up to date.

In any event the firm should have a procedure where money due to the practice is chased up. There can be a standard procedure where all clients are reminded (without reference to the partner or fee earner) that their bill is outstanding at the end of the first month after it was delivered. This can have a salutary effect on those partners or fee earners who deliver bills to achieve target with no prospect of them being paid within four weeks.

Further, there will be some partners or fee earners who are worse than the others at collecting their bills. Any time used to chase clients for outstanding money should therefore concentrate on those owing the most and from whom it is easiest to recover them. If the client does not pay at the end of the first month the fee earner or partner should be required to telephone the client to find out why. If that produces no result then proceedings should be commenced to recover the bill. If there is no prospect at all of being paid, the bill should be written off. Where an account has been unpaid for over six months then the VAT can be reclaimed. It is necessary to notify the client, however, as he or she will undoubtedly have claimed the VAT in relation to the bill disallowed in his or her return as an input.

At the practice's year end it is good housekeeping to assess the bills that are to be written off. The fee earners and partners will have been given the details of the bills and can therefore identify those which are unlikely to be paid. It is after all unnecessary to pay tax on fees which are unlikely to be paid.

As a matter of discipline it ought not to be possible to spend any money on clients by way of disbursements without having received payment from the client first. Clients are these days used to paying moneys on account.

If a record of the bills and disbursements is retained and produced once a month it is possible to see which fee earners and/or partners are the worst offenders. Those partners and fee earners need to be taken to task and be asked to account for any discrepancies. If the problems continue, more serious consideration needs to be given to the individual involved. After all one can play for nothing as work for nothing.

One reason why the bills outstanding can grow is the tension between getting cash in and achieving forecast. This is particularly true at the year end if there are bonuses to be gained. This is why bonuses should be related to cash receipts not bills delivered.

No allowance has been made in the cash forecast for disbursements which might arise. This is because it is intended that all disbursements will be funded by the clients. It will be readily appreciated that if this does not occur then the overdraft will go up or the bank balance will go down. "No-win-no-fee" agreements have already been mentioned. If this is a new step for the practice it is essential that the practice looks at the likely effect of all the funding coming from the partnership. Even a modest amount of business can generate a substantial amount of funding. If that or some other type of work which might create a similar problem is contemplated, it is essential that the figures are worked through.

To illustrate some of the points discussed above let us have a look at the cash flow forecast for Bowles, Green & Howes.

Tables 6 to 9 contain the figures to arrive at the cash flow forecast for the practice the subject of this book.

Taking the figures in this book, if the forecast turnover is £2,061,250 and the outstanding bills and disbursements on the balance sheet are £324,581 then this represents 57 days for the average bill to be paid. That figure is calculated by dividing the fees by 365, then dividing the resulting figure into the balance sheet figure for the bills and disbursements outstanding (£2,061,250/365 = £5,647; £324,581/£5,647 = 57 days). In many practices this figure can be over 80 to 100 days. The control of debtors is discussed earlier in the chapter.

The 57 days of the £2,061,250 does not represent cash, but money owed to the practice. It is necessary therefore to apply some discount to the actual fee receipts every month to arrive at a likely figure for the cash, that is actually going to be received. It is not as simple as deducting approximately £27,048 from the forecast for each month, (£324,581/12). As explained earlier, if the business has been running for some time each month it will be receiving payments for bills delivered 57 days before. As the fees will hopefully be growing it will be necessary to make an inspired guess at a likely figure. Before that can be done, however, it is necessary to consider the effect of VAT.

The figures for the likely bills do not take into account bills unpaid and VAT. Table 7 takes the annual figure, adds VAT and deducts 5% as discussed in the text. This gives a total of £2,300,870 as the anticipated cash receipts.

It is then necessary to consider the expenses. Table 8 sets out all the expenses which have been agreed in the budget. They appear under each month from May to April and have by and large been extrapolated on a straight line basis. There are one or two anomalies. For example the Christmas bonus has been added to the wages for December.

There appears to be an anticipated period when temporaries may be needed in July, August and February. If the practice knows that there may be difficulties during the year (maternity leave; holidays) then it clearly makes sense to make allowances for that. If the department could absorb the difficulty in the short term, of course, this might be a better way of dealing with the problem.

The average in each month is around £133,000. The difficulties with expenses are that these are known outgoings and not a lot can be done about them if the budget has been prepared sensibly.

Table 6 shows how the practice anticipates its bills will be delivered by the various departments and the branch office over the next 12 months. Some attempt has been made to see if there is any seasonal flux. The fees for the litigation department are higher at the end of the calendar year. The fees for conveyancing and the commercial department are extrapolated on the basis of a steady growth throughout the practice year (i.e. 30 April 2001).

However the figures are arrived at they can only be a best guess. Over the years and with experience they will become more accurate. The bottom line for Bowles, Green & Howes shows an average receipt of £172,000.

The numbers in Table 6 have had VAT added to each month and 95% of the total figure appears in each month in Table 9.

Table 8, which shows detailed expenses, also contains a reference to Depreciation and Interest received. Depreciation is not cash, so that while it is an expense to be considered for the purposes of the profit and loss account, it is not an outgoing for cash purposes. Interest on clients' accounts could appear in the fees figure. It has however been deducted from the expenses. If you total the two figures for depreciation namely £26,250 and £11,850 and add the interest of £34,500 you get £72,600. If you divide that by 12 you get £6,050. It is that figure which has been deducted from the expense totals each month to arrive at the expenses figure in the cash flow forecast.

The other items that need to be deducted are the drawings actually to be made by the partners; and the anticipated income tax, if the firm is continuing to underwrite the tax liabilities of the partners. (If the firm is not proposing to do that then the drawings will have to be increased by the anticipated tax liability so that the partners can save towards their own tax bill.)

Table 9 also shows a deduction for the partners' car expenses. If there are other expenses that will ultimately be debited to the partners but which are being withdrawn monthly by agreement, those figures need to be included as well.

The VAT payment dates are known and will represent the VAT on the bills delivered from the forecast and the VAT on bills from the previous year. Also deducted from that figure is any input tax which the practice has paid during the same period.

Income tax is payable in January and July.

When all the figures are tabulated, each column is added up to reveal the total cash payments anticipated over the period. It is this figure which is deducted from the anticipated discounted fees.

In May, therefore, £147,293 is anticipated by way of fees and £150,110 is anticipated by way of expenses. In May the expenses exceed the receipts so that, as the practice started with an overdraft of £244,726 it will be increased by £2,817, being the difference.

In the following month the position is even worse because VAT of £62,008 has to be paid. The overdraft then becomes £271,802.

The same calculations are made across the statement and it will be seen that the overdraft is at its worst in July at −£349,055. By the end of the year it is down to £200,916, an improvement over the period of £43,810 (£244,726 − £200,916). Clearly the position is not very satisfactory. If there is an error of £3,650 in each month then there will be no improvement. (£43,810/12).

Given that the forecast is no more than that, the actual figures may work out better. It will be necessary to keep a careful eye on the budget and forecast on a monthly basis, as an error of £3,650 in any month is not great. It might even be worthwhile going back to the forecast to see if any alterations could be made to improve the position.

Either way the forecast will create a discipline of keeping a tight control of expenditure in the office. If when comparing the actual figures with the forecast there is a divergence, it will be necessary to decide whether anything needs to be done or whether the cash will correct itself in the following month.

The results have been shown as a bar chart which in some ways shows the shape more easily. If a facility has to be agreed with the bank it would make sense to ask for £375,000 – to cover the peaks in July, August and September and to allow for some slippage.

It would be possible to improve the position if the bills outstanding were higher than the partners believed them to be. If, for example, the bills outstanding represented say 80 days, then for this practice that is effectively 20 days too much if the credit terms are 60 days. Twenty days at £5,647 per day represents £112,940. It would be worth the partners and fee earners doing nothing for one week other than chasing up outstanding bills!

How are you doing? Questions in relation to your practice and departments.

1. How many days of fees do your debtors represent?
2. What discount are you applying to the cash receipts for the purpose of the cash flow forecast?
3. Are there particular fee earners or partners whose bills and or disbursements are at an unacceptable level?
4. What do you propose to do about an unacceptable level of bills and disbursements?
5. Is your overdraft likely to rise or fall during the current year?
6. Is (your overdraft change) a result of trading conditions or is it planned?
7. Are you happy with the level of your overdraft?
8. Are you happy with the level of the capital accounts?

CHAPTER 4
THE BALANCE SHEET, PROFIT AND LOSS ACCOUNT AND TAXATION

> "Oh, I only look at my capital account; as long as it hasn't gone down I really don't need to know about the rest of it."

It is difficult for those of us who are unfamiliar with double entry book keeping to follow the ramifications of the balance sheet. For every entry on the balance sheet there is a corresponding entry elsewhere in the books of the business. For example, the profit from the profit and loss account appears in the capital accounts of the partners. The total of the money owed by the practice appears under creditors. The money due to the practice from clients, as fees and disbursements, appears under debtors.

The balance sheet only reveals the financial position of the office on a specific day. It is extremely important, however, because it identifies whether there has been any added value. At the end of the current year the practice must have advanced in value. That is, all the profit must not have been paid out as drawings to the partners, but some must have been retained to increase the net worth of the business. That increase will appear in the partners' capital accounts. The added value must however be just that. There is little point in increasing the value of the capital in the practice if the partners have lived in penuary during the year! If the amount of capital employed in the business is going down, eventually the bank will ask the partners to put more money in. Similarly, if the capital accounts and money in the business are increasing, the partners – whose capital accounts are going up – will look to take their money out, on the basis that they can do something more worthwhile with it themselves, not least spend it!

Where to start? All practices have fixed assets. These represent:

1. The business premises if they are owned by all or some of the partners.

2. Fixtures and fittings – soft furnishings, desks, chairs, pictures, etc.
3. Office equipment – computers, photocopiers, accounting machinery, etc.
4. Motor vehicles.
5. Goodwill.
6. Work-in-progress.

FIXED ASSETS

BUSINESS PREMISES

It may not be a good idea for a partnership to own its business premises. This is principally because office premises tend to have been acquired by one or more partners at different times in their careers. As a result the value appears in the balance sheet at differing amounts in their capital accounts. Those partners with property quite properly want a return on their investment, either in the form of rent or as interest. More often than not the additional monies are taken out as an increase in profit share as this is more tax effective. Rent is not allowed when assessing the amount that can be invested in a pension fund. Interest can vary with base rate making for difficult calculations. An additional share of profit can, in time, become divisive with the other partners who were not parties to the original arrangements.

One view is that, where property is disproportionally owned by various partners, it is better to take it out of the balance sheet altogether. Then it can be arranged for all the partners to lease the premises on a commercial basis from those partners who own the property.

A disadvantage may be that the value of the property comes off the balance sheet, which can lead to more capital being injected to make it balance. This does put some realism into the equation, however, and makes the partners realise just how much capital might be needed. It also removes the concern about a disproportionate share of the profits going to the property-owning partners.

FIXTURES AND FITTINGS

These speak for themselves. The balance sheet will, in a note to the accounts, show the value of purchases and disposals if any. Further, they will be depreciated at a constant rate. The rate depends on the perceived life of the item but is usually at a fairly low level, say 10% to 15% of their value.

OFFICE EQUIPMENT

This relates to equipment that has been bought by the practice. As explained earlier it will not include leased items. These are accounted for in the profit and loss account as an expense. No figure appears on the balance sheet for their actual capital value. Their capital value can be horrendous, when compared with the outright purchase of the same piece of equipment. Many solicitors will be familiar with the problems that arose when renting photocopiers. Different partners often dealt with the salesman and were talked into upgrades (with commensurate increases in the payment) for more up-to-date systems. Many found to their cost that they were locked into exorbitant repayment cycles. It is therefore important from time to time to work out the value of the office equipment which is being leased.

MOTOR VEHICLES

As mentioned when discussing the budget, there may be cars which the firm owns and allows either partners or staff to use. The present tax regime places a premium on such benefits and it is likely, where high mileage is involved, that it would make sense for the practice to increase salaries rather than provide cars or car allowances.

GOODWILL

Not many years ago retiring partners looked forward to receiving a payment for goodwill. Goodwill may represent the premium paid by them when they came into the practice. It can also represent any goodwill which might have been paid to other practices when the firm took over those practices.

It will be recalled that goodwill can only be of value if a practice is making a profit after deducting notional salaries from the bottom line profit. This "super profit" may only amount to 5% to 10% of the turnover. Some large commercial practices are producing 25% to 40% as a super profit. Clearly if they came to sell their practices they would be looking for a payment for that return. Valuing goodwill is not an exact science and is very dependent on the willingness of any purchaser to pay for it. If the business is making good "super profits" and has been operating for a long time from premises that it owns, it might be possible to achieve six to eight times their "super profit" as a value for the goodwill. If the business is producing less "super profit" it is likely that very little would be paid.

In a medium size firm it is unlikely that any value is placed on goodwill. These days many firms have enough difficulty getting good quality solicitors without expecting them to pay for goodwill. The argument raised by the successful firms is that, if a high share of profit is taken out on an annual basis, the partners must be satisfied with that. The partners must make their own arrangements for pensions and savings out of that profit. Goodwill like all other assets is depreciated on an annual basis. What the depreciation figure should be depends on its value. If the practice decides that it is not going to value goodwill it should say so in its partnership deed, so that the Capital Taxes Office cannot claim such a value on the death of a partner as liability to inheritance tax.

CURRENT ASSETS

WORK-IN-PROGRESS

Until recently many practices did not have any work-in-progress. This was because they had elected for their tax liability to be based on their bills paid and delivered. Work which had not been converted to fees was ignored. This had a cash flow benefit because tax was only payable on that work when it became a bill.

In April 2000 those practices without a work-in-progress value had to value work-in-progress for tax purposes and add the appropriate figure in the balance sheet. It was recognised that this would create a large tax bill, and it was agreed that the amount could be paid over ten years. Any subsequent tax on the increase in the work-in-progress from the previous year will be paid on that increase together with the the remaining balance of the tenth liability, calculated on the value of the work-in-progress agreed with the Inland Revenue for the purposes of the new legislation.

Work-in-progress does not include the value of the partners' work-in-progress. This is because that is considered to be profit and is only taken into account when the bill is delivered. The sudden increase in work -in-progress can artificially increase the value of the assets on the balance sheet and consequently the value of the partners' capital accounts. If there are partners who are retiring shortly, this will represent not only a boost to them but a substantial liability to the remaining partners.

Alternatively, the practice might take the view that as work-in-progress has never been taken into account in the past, it ought not to be now. As a result any work-in-progress credited to the partnership arising from the new provisions will be put into a separate account and will not be added to the partners' capital accounts. Further, no credit will be given to a retiring partner and no liability for payment will fall on the remaining partners. When income tax is assessed on the work-in-progress, it is debited to the separate account so that the capital accounts are not affected on the balance sheet. However, income tax still has to be paid and is a debit against the cash of the firm but not debited to individual partners. It will reduce, however, the amount of available cash that can be distributed between the partners. There are substantially different points of view when considering how to deal with the work-in-progress, that need to be resolved one way or another. How that has been or will be done by practices is something only they can decide. Interestingly the 1999 report from PriceWaterhouseCooper showed:

"There is obviously scope for firms to save potential tax charges by adopting appropriate valuation techniques. Those firms that did value work-in-progess at that date reported a wide range of valuations when expressed as a percentage of full selling price.

- 44% of firms valued work-in-progress at 25%, or less, of full selling price
- 29% of firms valued work-in-progress at between 26% and 50% of full selling price
- 17% of firms valued work-in-progress at betwen 51% and 75% of full selling price and
- 10% of firms continued to value work-in-progress in excess of 75% of full selling price.

Whichever percentage was agreed, the same percentage will have to be used for the future.

To the fixed assets must be added the rest of the current assets. These represent:

1. Debtors and disbursements outstanding.
2. Prepayments.

DEBTORS AND DISBURSEMENTS OUTSTANDING

Debtors have been discussed earlier and represent the amount of fees outstanding at the year end which may or may not get paid. It is possible to work out how many days on average it takes clients to pay. This is very useful information. Supposing the turnover is £3,000,000 then:

- In a year that equates to the practice billing at the rate of £8,219.18 per day (£3,000,000/365 days)
- If the debtors excluding disbursements outstanding are say £550,000 then this represent 67 days (£550,000/£8219.18)

Whether this is good enough depends on what the profession generally are doing. The disbursements should not be included as they do not form part of the turnover figure, and it is necessary when working out the figures to compare like with like. The disbursements could fluctuate enormously but might represent 25% to 30% of the bills outstanding. It is easy enough to find out as the breakdown of the bills outstanding on the computer should identify the disbursements for the same period.

There are many reports issued on a regular basis not only by the Law Society but also accountants and business consultants. BDO Stoy Hayward produced one such report in their report for the year 2000. Their survey is based on a relatively small number of firms who are members of the Law Society's Law Management Section and does not include the larger London practices. Their sample suggests that outstanding profit costs represents in the 5–10 partner firm a range between 26 days for the best and 54 for the worst. They add too that the days tied up in work-in-progress and the same group reveals 72 days at best and 170 days at worst. If the two are combined the figures are 117 days at best and 225 at worst. On any showing there is a tremendous variation from 90 days for the 2-4 partner firms to 225 days for some 5-10 partner firms. As they indicate – "there must be room for improvement".

It is important, therefore, to have a system which identifies the position with regard to bills outstanding and disbursements. Most practices these days expect clients to fund expenditure which relates specifically to them. If that is so, the disbursement figures should be reasonably easy to control. Certainly if the department heads or the individual partners and fee earners have to address their figures each month the controls should get better. A partner or fee earner can get away with the comment that "it will be paid shortly" in the first month, but they cannot do so in the next month. This accountability will make the partners anxious that they do not fall behind their colleagues and/or get singled out at the next meeting.

Bills outstanding can be broken down to the current bills, those more than three months old, and those which are over six months old. It is unlikely that a company or individual can be considered a client of the practice if they have a bill outstanding. They certainly will not instruct the firm again, because they know that as soon as they do so they will be asked to pay the outstanding account. If the client does instruct the practice while the fee is still outstanding, the old account should be discharged and it would make sense to get that client to pay something on account before doing any more work.

Rule 15 requires all firms to advise their clients of potential costs at the outset. It is also necessary every six months to advise clients if there is likely to be any change to those costs and the amount then owing. As a result of such notices it is open to the client to raise an objection. If he or she does not, the full bill has to be paid, and there is no good reason why it should not be. It must be remembered that clients have short memories. It is as well, not only to send the bill out as soon as the work is completed but also while the client still feels appreciative. The longer the delay in both sending the bill out and asking for payment, the harder it is to get payment. In fact the client will start to renegotiate the fee by suggesting that the job was not as efficiently done as you believed and that a discount would be a good idea. Often discount is agreed just to get a bill paid.

As has been pointed out earlier this effectively reduces the charge-out rate that was agreed at the beginning. For example, if the bill was £4,420 and represented 34 hours work at £130 a reduction of the bill by £750 represents £108 per hour. On that basis this partner or fee earner will not achieve his or her forecast if it is based on a charge out rate of £130. It has been established earlier that the partner or fee earner must charge more than his charge out rate on some matters to make up for those matters, like this one, where a reduction is sought. It is important to keep a check on the productive hours that partners and fee earners work, so that the conversion rate to fees is known. After all, if one or more partners continually discount their charge out rate either to keep the work or more likely because of their delay in billing and collecting their bills outstanding, it is as well to know. There is no point in having all this information if you do nothing with it.

If the bills outstanding represent a substantial number of days then it would pay to have the partner or fee earner involved spend some of his or her time contacting the clients and asking them to pay. Partners may not like doing this but it can be very effective. After all your bill outstanding is your client's cash at the bank. The client will be as anxious to keep it as you will be to get hold of it. If you don't ask for payment, the client will not normally volunteer to pay!

From the figures above it has been shown that on a turnover of £3,000,000 the daily fees are £8219.18. If office policy is that all bills should be paid in say 60 days, the fact that they represent (on the hypothetical figures mentiones above) 67 days then the aditional 7 days represent £57,534 outstanding above the agreed figure (7 × 8219.18). If the partner could get that amount in over the next two months it would be equivalent to nearly half of one fee earner's fees for the full year – and paid in cash. Surely it must be worth the effort.

For more on this, see EMIS Professional Publishing's *Credit Management for Law Firms* (see page 164).

PREPAYMENTS

These represent payments of the practice's expenses that have been paid in the current year for the credit of the following year and which are therefore a debit on the balance sheet date. They represent a debit on next year's cash as they have been paid in advance. They are a debit because they represent money owing to the partners which, on the balance sheet, is balanced by the capital accounts.

CREDITORS

The current liabilities are deducted from the current assets and identify the liquidity of the firm. If for example the creditors are greater than the debtors, the business must keep trading to pay off its creditors. Conversely if debtors and prepayments are greater than the creditors, then if the business had to close down it would have sufficient money to pay off its creditors. A similar calculation can be done for creditors as has been done for debtors to identify the number of days it takes to pay creditors. If the firm believes it pays its creditors in 30 days, the figure in the balance sheet should represent 30 days. It is possible to work out the average of creditors using the same calculations as for debtors. In arriving at the gross expenses it is necessary to deduct all those payments which have to be made at once. The most obvious item is wages. There will be others and it is necessary to work through those until you are left with a net figure. Suppose that the total overhead cost is £575,000 after making those deductions, then this represents £1,575.34 per day. If the creditors are £87,000 this represents 55 days on average (£575,000/365 = £1,575; £87,000/£1,575 = 55 days).

Some practices might seek to improve their cash position with the bank by extending the time it takes them to pay their creditors. The rationale is that, as the practice has to wait over 60 days for its bills to be paid, it is not unreasonable to expect the people to whom it owes money to wait that long as well. This is not a good idea. The problem with extended credit is that it may be necessary to pay an account when you are least able to. If it is decided to extend the payment cycle for creditors to say 80 days, for example, this is often because the fee income has slowed down. If the fees continue to be slow, it will not be possible to reduce the level of creditors. It only needs one creditor to begin proceedings for the liability to put pressure on the practice. It should be noted, however, that if extended time is taken to pay creditors then the overdraft, if there is one, will go down by that saving. This has the advantage that the amount of overdraft interest will also go down. The firm needs to be confident, however, that the fees will continue to rise and that the creditors can be paid sooner if the necessity arises.

The figures in the balance sheet identify these situations so that the practice can be aware of them and hopefully do something about them. It is for this reason that the quarterly accounts should include an updated balance sheet. At least then the partners will know whether the shape of the practice is changing and if so whether it is for better or worse. In either case the practice needs to identify the reasons for the change so that they can either use them to their advantage or change the way in which the practice operates.

Creditors include accruals. Accruals are the other half of prepayments. They represent the amounts which are due to creditors up to the year end, but will not actually be paid until after it.

TAXATION

All practices now pay tax under self-assessment on the current year's profits. Tax is payable on 1 January and 31 July. The tax liabilities of the partners are personal to them. Partners are no longer jointly and severally liable for their colleagues' tax liabilities. Most practices are still saving for the tax liability so that individual partners' tax can be met. The tax in January represents one half of the tax liability for the current year plus the balance of any tax not paid on the 31 July of the previous year, because that final amount was not known. If the tax is not paid on the due date, a penalty of £100 is incurred. Similarly the self-assessment form must be returned by the due date. The Inland Revenue will agree to waive the penalty if there is a "reasonable excuse". The only problem is that the reasonable excuse must be continuing. If the tax return is received in May of the current year it need not be sent until 1 January in the next year. If you want the Inland Revenue to work the tax out for you, the return has to be sent to them by 30 September. The individual amounts of tax appear in the note to the partners' capital accounts.

Quite frequently the Inland Revenue makes special rules for capital allowances. These are usually created to encourage businesses to incur a specific expense in the current year; for example, 100% tax allowance in the year of purchase when a computer is bought. You will recall that the expenses referred to depreciation. This is a notional amount to allow an annual saving for a piece of equipment so that it can be replaced in due course. If 100% capital allowance is to be given, then the depreciation figure is added back and the capital allowance figure substituted. This does not appear on the balance sheet except within the tax computation. The effect of the allowance is to reduce the tax bill for the year in question.

The individual's tax bill can be effected by the purchase of a pension. Quite frequently partners do not know how much pension they will purchase in any one year until after the year end, when they know their actual income and tax liability. If they subsequently decide to purchase some pension, all or a proportion of that cost will be allowed against their tax bill. The Inland Revenue no longer refunds tax overpaid by reason of a pension payment, but it does allow the payment as a deduction in the next tax payment by that partner. This means that if the partner has not increased his drawings the reduced tax liability will appear as an increase in his capital account

VAT

VAT does not appear in the balance sheet, nor does it appear in the profit and loss account. It is appropriate to discuss VAT in general terms at this point but a detailed explanation is outside the scope of this book. As has been seen it is taken into account in the cash flow forecast.

VAT is added to all fees from the practice except those related to exempt supplies. The principal exempt supply will arise in those practices that have a financial services department. In those circumstances it is necessary to apportion some of the expenses related to the financial services department, as those expenses are not allowed in any claim to input tax in that department.

Legal services are generally chargeable to VAT at the standard rate, this may not be the case where the supply is outside the UK. The Law Society has issued guidance on the steps to be taken before treating a supply as outside the UK. Otherwise VAT is due from the date when the supply of the services is completed. It is not always easy to know when that occurs, but VAT is payable in any event from the date a payment is received, or when a VAT invoice is issued. Alternatively an invoice can be is issued within 14 days of completion and the invoice date is treated as the completion date. The 14 day rule is extended to three months where a fee is not ascertained or ascertainable at the time the work was completed. This usually occurs when bills have to be taxed. Where payments are made on a retainer basis there may well not be a point at which the work is completed. In those circumstances VAT becomes chargeable from the date of the invoice.

Where payments are made specifically for the client, they are treated as disbursements and are not added on to the solicitor's bill for VAT purposes. Expenses which are incurred in providing the services are subject to VAT and cannot be treated as disbursements. Even telephonic transfers made on behalf of the client are subject to VAT.

OVERDRAFT

If you have a cash flow statement, an overdraft in the balance sheet should not be a surprise. It represents the figure which appears in the cash flow forecast and is updated at the end of each month, so that the actual figure can be compared with the forecast figure and appropriate action taken. More importantly, you will be able to see if it has gone up or down compared with the previous year.

The figure can be deceptive and should not be taken at face value. For example a VAT payment might be due at the year end but may not have gone through the bank account until the following day. VAT can represent a substantial sum of money. Conversely there may be a large fee expected that is not paid until the day after the year end, so that it may not appear in the current year's profit and affects the overdraft position.

The size of the overdraft is also affected by the level of drawings by the partners. If partners are drawing less cash than the profit being generated, the overdraft will go down and the capital accounts will go up. If, however, partners are drawing out more cash than the profits earned, the overdraft will go up and the capital accounts will decrease. Any overdraw of a partner's share of profits must be debited to that partner's capital account.

It is not uncommon for a partnership to decide to convert some of its overdraft into long-term borrowings. This has the effect of requiring not only an interest payment but a capital repayment schedule. As a result more cash may be going out to service the loan. If the partnership does not improve its profitability, it will find the overdraft moving up again. It is essential to ensure that the overdraft is maintained at a level that can be funded without the partners having either to reduce their drawings, or introduce more cash, or even both.

It is essential to generate sufficient profits to hold or reduce the overdraft and to increase the capital accounts so that the practice is moving forward. If there is no added value, there may not be enough surplus to allow the firm to progress and to allow for the movement of partners as senior ones retire and the younger ones come in.

When the first edition of this book came out in 1975 very few practices had overdrafts. Interestingly enough in their 2000 survey BDO Stoy Hayward reveals that in a 5-10 partner firm office bank balances run from –£141,169 to a credit balance of £112,352. The figures are even more startling for the practices with 11-125 partners. The sample reveals –£315,000 at the lower end and +£223,000 at the other.

HIRE PURCHASE CREDITORS

As explained earlier where equipment is bought on hire purchase the outstanding balance appears on the balance sheet as money owed by the practice to a third party. If the equipment is leased, it will not appear on the balance sheet but will appear as an expense in the profit and loss account. Lease arrangements do have penalties for early repayment which might arise if you want to replace the equipment. It is helpful to know what the actual value of the leasing arrangements are. This will help the practice to decide whether they wish to lease the equipment in the future or would prefer to buy it outright.

The total of the creditors is deducted from the current assets to give a negative or positive figure. If the figure is minus then it means that the practice has to keep trading to pay its debts. Clearly if this is very negative the bank may want some comfort from the partners by the introduction of further capital. The liquidity of the practice is important and the net current liabilities ought not to exceed the net current assets. If possible they should cover the liabilities with a reasonable amount to spare. It should be possible to have the current liabilities covered at least once by the current assets.

The resultant figure is deducted from the fixed assets and represents the total assets less the current liabilities.

There are usually further creditor payments which are not due except by installments in the current year. These will normally be:

1. Mortgages and/or bank loans other than the overdraft.
2. Hire purchase payments still due.
3. Capital due to others than a partner.

The mortgages and longer term bank loans are fixed borrowings often secured on the properties of the business. Hire purchase loans are the balances outstanding at the balance sheet date. It may be that a partner has left additional monies in the practice which appear as a loan, or a widow is entitled to a pension and has a balance of capital due to her. If so these figures will appear at this point in the balance sheet.

TOTAL ASSETS

These items are deducted from the last figure of assets less liabilities and the resultant figure represents the assets in the business at the balance sheet date.

This figure is balanced by the partners' capital accounts.

The individual capital accounts, that appear as a note to the accounts, are made up of:

1. The balance on the account from the previous year, positive or negative.
2. Any interest credited to or charged against the share of capital.
3. That partner's share of the profits for the current year.
4. There are then deducted the partner's drawings both the standing order he or she takes on a monthly basis and any additional cash withdrawn during the period.
5. Finally his or her tax liability is deducted leaving a balance at the end of the year.

Partners' capital accounts ought not to be negative. This can occur where there has been an overdraw. It is usual in those circumstances for that partner to have to pay interest on this overdraw. Frequently partnerships provide that the partners should have a fixed capital liability of say £25,000 to £50,000. Their current account might be negative from time to time and it is that account which gives rise to the interest charge. Similarly, another partner may not be drawing out all his or her income because he or she doesn't need it. As a result his or her current account increases and there is no need to put any further capital into the fixed capital account. He or she can then either draw the money out or receive interest on it. After all, while it is in the business the other partners are not having to borrow any further monies from the bank. It might be that the practice would prefer not to make a substantial payment at this time. If it is not possible to make a one off payment then that partner's drawings should be increased to allow the correction. It is not a good idea to allow partners' accounts to become too high.

The profit for the year is the amount credited to the partners' capital account as their share of the profit for the current year. What the share is depends on the agreements between the partners. The most common arrangements are that the practice allows the partners to move up the partnership with an increase in their share of the profit basically calculated to the time he or she has been in the practice.

There can be an inequality in relation to drawings. Some partners then take out their projected share of the profits from the budget and forecast less an agreed discount (say 15%); this allows for slippage and their income tax liability. Some firms may then allow payment of miscellaneous accounts for partners; repairs insurance; petrol for the partners' own cars; telephone bills; newspapers and periodicals; memberships of clubs, etc. Some partners may also pay their own standing orders for, say, the lease of their cars through the firm. It is important that the partnership is aware of the variations and agrees them, otherwise partners can be receiving advantages that their colleagues are not getting and that can be divisive.

The tax liability is deducted and the end figure represents that partner's balance on his current and fixed capital accounts. It is this figure in the balance sheet that most partners look at. If it is larger than the previous year (but not by too much) the accounts are then put in a drawer and forgotten. If the figure is less than the previous year, the same thing occurs but that partner hopes that nobody will raise any queries with regard to it. Both partners should be more proactive, study the accounts and draw the appropriate conclusions. If in doubt they should arrange to see the firm's accountants to explain the accounts to them.

When you next look at the balance sheet you should check several points.

- The level of debtors. If the number of days outstanding has increased from earlier months, there will be an opportunity to improve the cash flow. It may be that one of the partners or fee earners is not collecting his or her fees efficiently.

- The level of creditors. If the figure has gone down it may be that creditors are being paid too quickly. There would be an opportunity to increase the cash at bank by slowing down the payments.

- Bank overdraft. Is this increasing for business reasons or are the partners drawing out more than they are forecast to make.

- Capital accounts. See if any overdrawing is occurring. (The most likely time for the figures to go adrift will be in July when tax is paid.)

- If the current assets are less than the current liabilities, the practice is clearly heading for difficulties as the liquidity is not satisfactory. (In other words, it cannot pay its bills out of its existing cash or near cash.) It may well be that the overall capital (i.e. the amount of assets credited to the partners as a whole) is satisfactory, because it is represented by the value of the properties. However, the partnership could not countenance selling the properties if there was insufficient cash to pay the on-going liabilities.

Table 10 shows the balance sheet for the previous and current year for Bowles, Green & Howes. Attached to it are notes (Table 11) explaining some of the balances.

Table 10 Bowles, Green & Howes balance sheet as at 30 April 2001

	Notes	2001	2000
Fixed Assets			
Tangible assets	1	1,039,302	1,009,171
Goodwill	2	25,864	28,736
		1,065,166	1,037,907
Current Assets			
Work-in-progress		145,000	125,000
Debtors and disbursements advanced		325,540	438,581
Prepayments		47,250	52,200
		517,790	615,781
Creditors			
Amounts falling due and payable within one year			
Creditors and accruals		100,458	150,280
Bank overdraft		215,916	315,000
Hire purchase creditor		41,358	38,700
		357,732	503,980
Net Current assets/liabilities		160,058	111,801
Total assets less current liabilities		1,225,224	1,149,708
Creditors			
Amounts falling due and payable more than one year			
Bank Loans	3	661,666	694,832
Hire purchase creditor		8,500	9,200
		670,166	704,032
		555,058	445,676
Financed by			
Partners Capital accounts	4	425,058	325,676
Work-in-progress		130,000	120,000
		555,058	445,676

Tangible assets have increased to £1,039,302. The note indicates that there have been additions of £35,000 to the branch office. The office had the opportunity of adding some additional rooms from adjoining property and the partners took the view that they should take advantage of the opportunity as it might not come up again. They considered that it was a cheaper option than having to move at a later date.

Table 11 Bowles, Green & Howes notes to accounts

	Principal Office	Branch Office	Fixtures Fittings	Office Equipment	Total
1. Fixed Assets					
Cost					
At 30th April 2000	566,502	292,360	81,007	69,302	1,009,171
Additions		35,000	23,750	7,741	66,491
	566,502	327,360	104,757	77,043	1,075,662
Depreciation			20,951	15,409	
	566,502	327,360	83,806	61,634	1,039,302

2. Goodwill

Cost	30th April 2000	28,736
	Depreciation at 10%	2,872
	Balance at 30th April 2001	25,864

3. Bank loans and mortgages

A loan of £800,000 was advanced by the Nationwide Building Society on 20th August 1990 repayable over 25 years secured on the principal office. Balance outstanding £480,000

A loan of £275,000 was advanced by HBSC on 14th May 1995 repayable over ten years secured on the property at Old Hall (the Branch office). Balance outstanding £137,500

The overdraft loan was converted in part to a fixed term loan over 15 years on 15th October 1998
The loan is unsecured and the balance out standing is £44,166

4. Capital Accounts

	Balance at 1/5/00	Interest at 5%	Profit	Drawings	Tax	Balance at 30/4/01
A Green	42,000	2100	71,000	53,500	16,500	45,100
S Howes	38,000	1900	68,000	48,000	14,575	45,325
T Kirkby	32,000	1600	59,000	50,000	11,250	31,350
etc:						
	325,676	21000	502,292	283680	140230	425,058
Work In Progress	120,000					130,000
	445,676					555,058

THE BALANCE SHEET, PROFIT AND LOSS ACCOUNT AND TAXATION

There has been some considerable money spent on office furniture and some more computer equipment has been acquired. These items have been discounted at 10% hence the balancing figure. It will be recalled that there is a favourable capital allowance regime which will allow 100% of the expense on computers. The properties have not been depreciated as it is considered that they will have increased in value. It will be remembered that if there is a change in the partnership it will be necessary for the properties to be revalued.

Goodwill is being depreciated at 10% per annum. This is an historical figure which arose when the practice bought the branch office from a sole trader five years ago.

These partners have decide to create a balance sheet figure for work-in-progress. The work-in-progress figure will vary from year to year. Where it is not included in the partners' capital accounts, it will have set against it the year-on-year tax liability. The figure will help with the bank, however, in revealing the actual value of the work-in-progress each year and increasing the bottom line value on the balance sheet, as long as the work in progress figure goes up.

The partners were concerned that the debtors were running at too high a level in the previous year and have had a purge. Some of the debts have been written off. These amounted to £40,000 in the current budget the reduction of a further £73,000 has been achieved by persuading the partners and fee earners to be more rigorous in control of billings and requests for disbursements.

The creditors and accruals have been reduced principally because the partners have taken in-house an individual to look after the computers, which has effectively reduced the maintenance charge and rationalised the computer spend.

The overdraft is down because the partners have not increased their drawings, so the profit is at a greater level than those withdrawals. If the partners had drawn out more than the forecast profit, the capital accounts would have gone down. You can reorganise the balances in the balance sheet as much as you like, as long as you stay within the same section of the balance sheet. For example, if the firm decided to hold back a further £50,000 of creditors, creditors would go up by £50,000 and the overdraft would come down by the same amount. The capital accounts are unaffected.

The liquidity of the practice was unsatisfactory in the previous year as creditors exceeded current assets by £8,199. The position is now better, and liquidity has improved by nearly £38,000 (£30,058 + £8,199).

The note for bank loans show what they consist of. Not surprisingly they relate to the purchase of the two properties by the partners. There was also a refinancing of the overdraft which is unsecured.

The total of £425,058 is balanced by the partners' capital accounts. These are shown as a note to the accounts. The figures for the three original partners are shown, the other partners' figures will be extrapolated in the same way and the bottom line shows all the additions.

This practice has decided to create a balance sheet reserve for the work-in-progress. The balance appears with the capital accounts of the partners, and represents the net figure after the payment of the one tenth tax bill for the current year and the tax on the increase of the work-in-progress from the previous year.

How are you doing? Questions in relation to the balance sheet.

1. Is your property owned by some or all of the partners? If the former, should it be?

2. Is there a value for goodwill? If so, what is it and should it be written off?

3. Are the debtors and disbursements being properly monitored? How many days' fees do they represent and is this satisfactory?

4. Are you paying your creditors on time? How many days' credit are you taking?

5. Is your bank overdraft at a reasonable level?

6. Is it possible to refinance the bank loans by extending the period of the loans; reducing the interest charge; borrowing in euros?

7. Are the capital accounts satisfactory? If not, are some partners' accounts too high and others not high enough?

CHAPTER 5
COMPUTERS

"I have a computer on my desk, but I only use it to read my email. I really need a five-year-old to explain it all to me."

Looking back through earlier editions of this book it is surprising to note how quickly computers have taken over the office environment. Mention in earlier texts identifies computers as either wordprocessors or spreadsheets. Either use was separate and operated through stand-alone machines. The problem these days is the multiplicity of choice. The choice lies not only within the machines themselves but in the various programs which can be run on them. To see how EMIS Legal can help, see page 163.

DEFINITIONS

Let us start with some basic definitions.

Hardware	The physical computer and monitor and associated peripherals, e.g. printer, scanner, modem.
Software	The programs that run on the computer.
Word processor	Software used to type documents, save them on the computer or to a back-up system and amend at will, producing hard copy to a printer whenever required. It usually includes additional utilities like spell check, grammar check and a basic thesaurus.
Spreadsheet	Software normally used to facilitate the manipulation of numbers and produce lists of information, for example the preparation of Estate Accounts (it will do the calculations for you if the correct formula is entered). You use a grid of boxes (known as cells), each of which can contain discreet information or perform calculations based on information contained in other cells.

Stand-alone	A computer that is not connected to any other computers.
Network	A group of computers connected to each other to share information. Within a building the computers are normally connected by copper cabling. Between buildings computers can be connected by using telephone lines, fibre optic cable, microwave frequencies.
Internet (aka The World Wide Web)	A world-wide group of computers linked together, normally by use of the telephone network.
Surfing the web	Looking for information on the internet, either by typing in the name of the website you wish to look at (e.g. www.BowlesGreen&Howes.co.uk) or by searching using a search engine (e.g. Yahoo, Alta Vista, Lycos)
Modem	A piece of hardware attached to your computer that allows it to communicate with the telephone network, and therefore access the internet.
Email	Electronic mail – software that allows you to send and receive messages and documents electronically. Usually faster than normal post!
Scanner	A piece of hardware that will copy photographs or documents on to your computer. Using OCR (Optical Character Recognition) software you can scan a document and translate it to text so you can then edit it, rather than just having a picture of it.
Backup	Taking copies of the software and data on your computer on to floppy disk or tape. You can then restore information that is lost.
CD ROM	A compact disk, similar to that used for music, but storing data or software.

Egton, EMIS's hardware sister company, provides a free IT glossary: see p.164.

WHAT IS AVAILABLE?

A stand-alone system incorporating computer, screen, keyboard, printer and scanner can be purchased from a high street retailer for less than £1000 (specialist sellers such as Egton can have prices as low as £500). Whether more expensive machines are required depends on what they are going to be used for. A small practice can probably manage very well with individual machines on each desk with word processing software installed. With this alone, very sophisticated documentation can be produced.

WORD PROCESSING

Using a word processor the operator can create a document from scratch and save it. It can then be printed out and sent to another solicitor for comment, or even sent by email. If and when a draft is approved, the appropriate amendments can be made to the original saved on the computer and the engrossed document produced ready for signature.

The introduction of word processors and the accompanying ease of amendment has had the effect of lengthening documents. However, there is no excuse for spelling or grammatical errors as many of the word processing applications now include spelling and grammar checks. It isn't much fun receiving such a document as it takes a very long time to check through and make sure that it is right. Make sure you do read documents thoroughly, however: spelling checks alone are not satisfactory, they recognise words not sense.

PROBLEMS

Two fairly obvious problems tend to occur with documents produced on computer:

1. A failure to mark on the draft the name and location of the document so that it can be easily retrieved.
2. A failure to read the entire text to ensure that it is correct.

Identifying the document in a footnote at the bottom of the page enables it to be easily found if the author is on holiday or unavailable. Footnotes are very useful, you can also include information such as the date the draft or engrossment was produced. However, the footnote must be updated each time there is a change or else the information is meaningless or worse, misleading.

Further, where text is produced as a precedent on a regular basis for the same client it is too easy for clauses to be incorporated from an earlier draft, when they are not appropriate. In this fast moving environment it is essential to check the document before it leaves the office.

BENEFITS

The obvious advantage of being able to save and reproduce text at a whim is that it can save an enormous amount of time. The same document can be used on another occasion, re-saved in its new format with a different name, without losing the original version. It is prudent to have a basic precedent, which can be amended to accommodate particular circumstances. In time, precedents created in this way can be stored centrally or on a disk and be made available as basic precedents for the practice as a whole. The publishers of legal precedents have recognised the benefit of this and have produced standard precedents on CD ROM to accompany their books or replace them. Such software can allow even the smallest practices to buy in prerecorded precedents to be reproduced to suit the particular occasion. Typically publishers issue updated versions of the CD ROMs periodically so that there is no reason for a practice to be out of date with its text. Knowledge management software can also ensure your own precedents are easily accessible (see page 163).

TYPING SKILLS

One of the principal reasons that fee earners and more particularly partners, do not take full advantage of a computer is that they are not typists! It would be splendid to achieve 190 words a minute, but not many aspire to or need that. Excellent results are possible using "hunt and peck" typing. While being able to touch type is a distinct advantage, it is not a requirement of using a computer or word processor. However, typing speed does increase with practice. Further, because of the sophistication of most software these days, it does take time to absorb the capabilities of any software application. Manufacturers of software are, of necessity, several years ahead of end users, and in order to maintain their position in the market need to develop and improve the software continually. A direct result of these improvements is that more and more powerful and memory–hungry machines are required over time. There is always something better about to happen, all of which increases the cost. It can be tempting not to get on the merry-go-round at all. However, unless you are able to produce documents with the speed and accuracy of your competitors, you will soon be left behind.

SCANNING

A scanner allows you to photocopy text and photographs effectively on to your computer. Using OCR software, a document drafted by other solicitors and not accessible directly by you, can be scanned into your computer and then edited.

The same hardware can be used for scanning photographs, until the digital camera takes over. Where clients have photographs of the state and condition of a building it is very useful to be able to incorporate those in the schedule in a document. The digital camera removes the need to scan a photograph as, with appropriate software, the photograph can be copied on to the computer directly from the camera.

TRAINING

Running in parallel with the introduction and use of computers is the need to train all who will be using them. This is not as easy as it sounds. Some people will not admit to their skills or lack of. Many of your staff may have computers at home and already be more familiar with the use of them than you are aware. You will need to identify the skills required for each group of people or department. These skills do not just include computer skills, but telephony, numeracy, literacy and client care. For example the accounts department will not need the speed-typing skills of an audio typist, but will need knowledge and understanding of basic accounting practice and the accounts software application. It is important to identify the computer skills required by partners and other fee earners. Many presently pass simple tasks to their support staff which, with training, they can easily complete themselves, for example typing a short file note, or sending emails. This releases the support staff to do the more complex tasks and improve efficiency.

UPDATING

Once you have embarked on the computerisation of your office, you will soon notice that computer systems frequently need updating. There are always new and improved versions of software, that in turn need more powerful computers to run them on. It is not always financially sensible or viable to embark on large scale "one hit" replacement programs. Therefore plan your change over a period of time and build in time for upgrades. A common practice is to replace PCs once they are three years old. While existing machines function adequately, you will find that you are soon unable to upgrade your software as your computers are unable to run it, or will do so but poorly. Also, while old versions of software still function adequately, suppliers remove support for a version of software within two or three years of its release. You may find yourself in a position where you wish to purchase a new printer, but the software that you are using is unable to communicate with it and therefore is unable to print. Using computers can be rather like painting the Forth Bridge, just as you think you've finished it will be time to start again.

When implementing new computer systems, it is helpful to have "champions" within each department. Champions are individual members of staff with a greater level of knowledge of the computer system than their colleagues. They are able to resolve simple problems, for example adjusting the brightness and contrast on a monitor, or selecting a different printer. This will release any in-house IT staff for more complex work, or reduce the cost of using a third party computer support helpline.

VOICE RECOGNITION

One aid to the use of computers on the horizon is "Voice Recognition". This is computer software that allows you to give instructions to the computer by talking to it. This can include you dictating letters to your word processor which will be typed on screen as you speak. From there you can amend the text as appropriate, save the document and print it. The obvious advantage is that the partner or fee earner can tell the machine what they want it to do.

Voice recognition systems are currently available but are still in their infancy. Sophisticated software will be able to interpret instructions from the user, without the user having to know how to access the information they require. For example, most beginners spend a fair amount of time finding their way around a new computer system, learning to use a mouse, identifying simple commands such as bold, italic and underline. With voice recognition software this time spent familiarising yourself with a new computer system is usually spent "teaching" the software your voice. A pronounced Geordie accent sounds entirely different to the broader Lancashire tones!

If all this can be achieved by merely talking to a machine, the ability to operate a computer becomes very straightforward. In the not too distant future it will be possible to talk to a computer from somewhere warm and sunny, via a mobile phone, and have the text typed in China and printed at your home ready for your return!

SPREADSHEETS

Spreadsheet software allows you to manipulate numbers. You can use them to do "what if" calculations, for example to investigate impact on the financial standing of the practice if a new department is formed or if the practice merges with another law firm.

Supposing the practice decided to establish an insolvency department. If you are looking to the department to make 30% net, enter the proposed staffing, estimated fee income and the necessary overhead costs to sustain the department into a spreadsheet. Using simple calculations you can see if your initial plan is financially viable and then manipulate the numbers to give you the best shaped department that will give the return required. Having done this, a commercial decision can be made as to whether all the variables are reasonable and whether the venture would be a success. Assuming that you decide to launch the department, actual fees and costs can be entered into the spreadsheet against the model to see if the assumptions were correct. In fact no commercial organisation would dream of setting up a new department not having first "run the numbers" and carried out appropriate market research to limit the margin for error.

The spreadsheet also lends itself to use in a probate department, as the estate account can be easily built up as the case progresses, with the result that the final accounts can be produced very easily.

NETWORKS

A computer is more than a sophisticated typewriter or wordprocessor. With the right software it can take over, or at least assist with, many of the mundane and repetitive tasks required in a legal practice, for example form filling. Linking computers together via a network or even the internet, allows them to communicate with each other and share resources, for example printers. Even simple email can improve communication and information flow around the practice. When sending documents between machines it is preferable for each machine to have the same software. However, this is not absolutely necessary as the recent versions of software are capable of reading documents created by their competitors.

In small offices it may not be necessary to link all the computers together by a network. Information can still be shared between machines by saving the document to a floppy disk and passing it between users (otherwise known as "sneaker-net").

In larger organisations it is more convenient to have systems that allow any number of machines to share centrally located information and communicate with each other. Most networks link all the computers to a central computer known as a server. It is the server that holds information, for example documents and client databases, rather than information being stored on each individual computer. It is therefore accessible to everyone within the practice, assuming the system administrator has given them access to the area of the server that the information is stored on.

BACKING UP

It is essential that a regular backup is taken of the data and software stored on the server, in case the server fails. Servers do fail occasionally, although they are remarkably stable given the amount of use. They fail most often when new software is installed. A proper discipline should be developed to make a backup copy of the information stored on the server. Backup is normally done using a specific piece of backup software and data are copied to a backup tape. More than one generation of backup tape should be kept so that should a backup fail you have older generations to fall back on. A good practice is to backup your system daily, keeping the tape used on each Friday for the month and the tape used on the last day of the month for 12 months. In this way you can recover information for the previous five days, each week or at the end of each month. Also ensure that you keep a recent copy of the backup off site; then should you be unable to access your building, you can retrieve information from the backup at another location.

STORAGE

While centrally stored information is a bonus, no machine has an infinite capacity to store data. Therefore you need to undertake regular "house-keeping" of the information stored, deleting anything that is no longer required. This is where backups stored for a period of time come into their own, as you can guarantee that you will delete something that you need to access in the future.

PROBLEMS

Most practices that use computers will have suffered the inevitable "crash" and will not have sufficient backup copies of the information in order to recover. Many practices do not have an agreed system to deal with the possibility of the entire computer system crashing. Planning for the loss of a key computer system not only involves recovering the information stored, but putting contingency plans in place so that the practice can continue to function while the system is repaired. This can include resorting to documented manual procedures, having individual computers with software installed so that users can continue to generate documents and relocating printers to be attached to individual machines rather than in a network. If a computer system fails without any of these contingencies in place you will not let it happen again!

USES OF NETWORK SYSTEMS

A network of computers has a myriad of applications in conjunction with the appropriate software. Most email software includes a diary function. This allows each user to have their own diary and email Inbox. It then becomes possible to book a meeting centrally and update each attendee's diary at the same time. Further information regarding the meeting can be sent directly to those attending. Overall communication becomes much easier, especially if you are not at your desk all day every day to answer the phone and reply to memos. However, even a modest number of email messages can take an inordinate amount of time to work through. Ensure that you check your email regularly throughout the day to be sure that you haven't missed anything important.

A central store of information can include:

1. A central register of experts for the office (and incidentally for Legal Aid compliance).
2. A central database by department or client which will facilitate targeted mail shots for invitations to seminars, newsletters.
3. A central register of undertakings to banks, building societies, other organisations and clients.
4. A central bank of precedents enabling individuals to access necessary draft documents. This also promotes a uniformity of style and presentation of documents through the office.
5. A central register of bills, allowing individuals to number bills sequentially, without referring to cashiers for each bill number.
6. An office manual, accessible by all parties and regularly updated.

It is possible to link different types of computer together on a network. Typically, this will give a member of staff access to the accounts computer to enquire on matter accounts before requesting disbursements be paid. This removes the need to ask cashiers the state of the client account before each cheque is requested, or each bill created. Most systems allow a printout from the screen of the client account, which can be kept with the client file if appropriate. Note that it is not always appropriate for non-cashiers to do anything but enquire on matter accounts.

There are software applications available which allow a fee earner to log the time spent on a matter directly to the client ledger. However, time recording systems are only as good as the people who normally fill in time sheets. Also, it may be necessary to record time spent on a matter on the file in addition to the client ledger. In a litigation matter, it may be that when you come to tax the bill you need to identify to the District Judge how the time was actually expended. While it may sound obvious, if during the budgeting process it is decided that time charges need amending, it is important that the correct information is passed to the accounts department so that the new rates are properly calibrated. Otherwise fees will be calculated at last year's rates!

THE INTERNET

Most of us are familiar with the internet, if only through the use of email. The internet allows a business to communicate with other organisations via email and through dedicated web-sites, which in turn also offer goods and services.

EMAIL

The use of email has speeded up legal work dramatically. Draft documents can be emailed between parties, amended, agreed and then engrossed in either solicitor's office. If a debenture is to be executed but all terms have not been agreed, they can be so agreed and then emailed for typing in the recipient's office. Further, where leases require photographs attached, they can be taken with a digital camera, downloaded on to the computer and sent by email to any number of recipients for printing and attaching to the lease. The possibilities are endless.

WEB SITES

Some services available to solicitors and the general public are outstanding. In a legal context several firms provide information on line on their web site (for a fee). Statutes, precedents, case law, articles, etc. abound. Some providers send selected information daily by email to partners and fee earners. For example, if you specialise in personal injury work then the organisation will update you on a daily basis in relation to all case and statute law that could affect you. They can also identify current trends in liability and quantum. The Law Society has recently launched their own web site listing all practising solicitors and their firms, their areas of specialisation, languages spoken and qualification for public funding. The web site is available to the general public free of charge. Users can find a solicitor in their area with the specialisations they require, and link to the solicitor's own website for further information.

The power of the internet is awesome and there is really no excuse for any solicitor not to be up to date. Also, be aware that clients also access the internet, and may already have a basic understanding of their problem. They will then expect you, their solicitor, to advise them in depth on the matter. Access to basic law is likely to become a "given". There are already organisations providing a lot of free basic legal documentation on their web sites. Much of this information can be saved to a users' own computer and reproduced by them. The technology and culture of the internet is already having a fundamental influence on the profession.

One consideration is to have your own web site. It should be appreciated that web sites are being added to the internet at a fantastic rate. There is so much information that sometimes "search engines" do not find all the answers. As a result, there are organisations who offer to do the searching for you. That is all very well, but it can mean a third party interfacing between you and your client, and receiving a fee for their trouble. This may cause a client-confidentiality problem and you may also lose the client. Web sites are discussed in more detail in Chapter 8.

There are two main problems that arise from the use of the internet – browsing and security. If everyone in the organisation has access to the internet, a great deal of time may be wasted looking at various non-work related sites. There are software applications which will filter the sites that can be accessed, based either on key words or web site addresses. It may be better to put a softer policy in place, giving general guidelines on use, stipulating whether the facility can be used for personal information and if there are restrictions on the times when this can be done and importantly prohibiting the use of the internet for illegal activities. If you wish, you can make inappropriate use of the internet a disciplinary matter, via an email policy.

The implications of the internet and ecommerce have not been fully absorbed by many practitioners. It is understood that some businesses are having their routine typing done in the Far East!

VIRUSES AND HACKERS

There has been much in the news about hackers accessing web sites and either defacing them or introducing "viruses" which can prove destructive. Hackers enjoy finding ways into computer systems not only to cause difficulties but to identify to the industry that the systems are not always as secure as they are made out to be. Your computers can be infected with a virus when accessing an infected site, or by receiving an infected email. The damage caused is dependent on the virus. Some just flash up a message on your screen, others delete all the information on your computer and render it unusable. Remember the earlier paragraph about backups? There are anti-virus software applications available. These are well recommended, but to be effective they must be updated on a regular basis.

AN IT STRATEGY

It can be seen from what has been said so far that computers and their potential use are somewhat complex. It is surprising therefore that practices, by and large, not only fail to have an IT strategy, but also fail to identify if the use of computers has either saved them money or produced an element of added value to the service provided. PriceWaterhouseCoopers' survey for 2000 reveals that "nine out of every ten firms have no idea as to what cost savings will be realised from their IT investment. This is probably because it is only recently that firms have started holding strategic meetings. In fact a third of all firms with less than 15 partners have no strategy at all" (see PriceWaterhouseCoopers' survey). If a practice has no business plan it is hardly surprising that there are few strategic plans for the use of computers. It is clearly necessary to have computer systems, but it is essential to decide how they are going to be used and at what cost. There are very few areas of expenditure that can run away with money to the extent that computers do.

The rationale for a computer system must be that, in the short to medium term, it can lead to efficiencies which will increase the volume and accuracy, that in the longer term will reduce or stabilise the wages bill. As wages appear on average to be running at 40% of turnover these days, it is important to ensure that the percentage does not increase. You will recall that the ideal shape for a practice is that wages should represent no more than 33% of turnover. The extra 7% can be accounted for by the need to have experts in-house to assist with running the practice. Such experts include dedicated computer staff.

If a business strategy is embraced, it ought to be possible to identify those areas within the office that can make best use of computers. As you will already have some computers in use, first identify the machines and software that are currently installed. Then decide if these are suitable for the departments and staff using them. For example, if the majority of your fee earners dictate their work to secretarial staff, then the secretarial staff need better performing computers.

DEDICATED SYSTEMS

Some departments may find software dedicated to a particular discipline suits them best. Others may just require an update to the current software and additional training in its use. In this latter case, decide on the level of skills required and train and test the users to ensure that the appropriate standard is achieved.

If a dedicated system is required, the practice needs to consider some, more or all of the following when choosing software:

1. What procedures are to be automated, for example the generation of standard letters on given target dates?
2. How much control is the user to have over the content of documents produced?
3. Does the software come with ready prepared precedents, or must they be input?
4. If you have a client database, can the information from this be downloaded to the new software, removing the need to re-input information?
5. Does the software work in conjunction with your existing software. For example, does it have its own word processing application or will it use yours and place information in the appropriate places in the documentation?
6. What do you want to achieve with the software now?
7. What will you want to achieve in the future?
8. Who will be using the software? This can affect the cost.
9. How much will it cost now?
10. Is there an annual charge for using it?
11. Does the company provide a helpline for problems using the application?
12. Is training included in the price?
13. Have you seen the software in action at another solicitors? What do they think about it? How easy do they find it to use?
14. Involve the people who will be using the software in the decision making process. While you often get what you pay for, the most expensive is not always the best suited to your needs.

By putting the effort in at the beginning, new software can be implemented easily, there are fewer nasty surprises and the staff will use it. There are probably quite a few dedicated systems in solicitors' offices which cost a small fortune and which have seldom or never been used!

The IT strategy needs to be documented and available to everyone to read. Write it in a format that is comprehensible to the lay partner and fee earner. Computer jargon is not readily understood. Neither is legal jargon to the lay person. Ideally the strategy should also identify timescales by which each phase should be completed.

The range of options available to you when considering computers are legion and have been discussed in some detail above. If you feel that the whole exercise is too much for you to handle, in time or knowledge, it makes sense to speak to a dedicated computer consultancy, preferably one used to dealing with solicitors and ask their advice. They may be able to find the most suitable system for you. While they cost money, they will probably save you getting it wrong. (See EMIS Legal, page 163 for one option.)

How are you doing? Questions in relation to computers.

1. Do you have an IT strategy?
2. Do you know what computers and software you are using?
3. Do you know how much in real terms the computers are costing you?
4. Do all the partners and fee earners have access to a computer? If so, do they know how to use them to their best advantage?
5. Do you have access to the internet?
6. Do you have a web site and if so what is it designed to do for you?

CHAPTER 6
MANAGEMENT, STAFF AND TEAMS

"Listen…" "I do listen…" – "to the end of the sentence!"

PARTNERSHIP DEED

To start at the beginning, the partners need to have a partnership deed. It is surprising how many practices do not have one. This (like all legal documents) will only be called in aid when things go seriously wrong. Until a major dispute arises, any difficulties will be dealt with by mutual agreement on a majority vote by the partners as they go along.

The deed ought to identify how the practice is to be run, but frequently does no more than identify that most decisions are to be made on a show of hands on a simple majority. Where the subject matter is fundamental to the partners, a three-quarters majority is normally required.

After that the partners are on their own. In a small partnership it is likely that one of the partners (usually the founding partner) acts as managing partner. Matters for discussion will be brought to all the partners and will normally be resolved on a simple vote. The founding partner is not necessarily the best person to run the practice in the longer term. The politics, however, dictate that he does!

There are principally three models of management for partnerships. The first is really no management but works on the basis that each of the partners does something, not infrequently overlapping an activity already being done by another partner! The second is a similar model, except that in this case there is a committee of two or three partners who take responsibility for running the practice. The third model is having a managing partner.

NO MANAGEMENT

In the first model the partners agree that they will split into groups, with each group responsible for certain parts of the office activities. The group will consider the appropriate problem and come back to a full partners' meeting for it to be discussed again and not infrequently, either shelved or referred back to the same group for further consideration. The degree of commitment from the partners determines the effectiveness and speed of action. From this it is clear that any partner can delay the making of any decision for some considerable time. This is particularly the case if he or she has discussed the matter with other partners before the meeting. As a consequence matters tend not to be resolved and essential decisions are delayed. In some circumstances matters tend to get worse as the market place moves on and smaller problems frequently never get solved. Partners' meetings tend to be very lengthy and not very conclusive.

Important issues are left and discussion take place with regard to non-controversial matters, because any decision arising from those do not effect the partnership fundamentally. There is frequently an unwillingness within the partnership to make the partners either **responsible or accountable.** This is usually because many of the partners, one way or another, have matters relating to their interests in the practice that they do not wish to discuss because such matters could affect them adversely. As a result the same partners do not wish to take issue with their colleagues, because they do not want to create any problems for themselves. That way no serious decisions need to be made.

MANAGEMENT BY COMMITTEE

In a practice of any size the first method of running the practice could be inefficient. In this model two or three of the partners form a committee which is responsible for running the practice. That committee in turn may delegate some of their functions to other partners. Where that is done these partners must be allowed to make decisions without having to keep coming back to the committee. Any of the management matters that are taken on must also be time bound. Timescales are a key requirement and if these are not strictly adhered to matters will tend not to get done. For example, if it is decided to have an IT strategy, a partner must have the responsibility to deliver that strategy. He or she needs to be given a financial framework to operate within. If there has been a budgetary exercise, as described earlier in this book, it will be known how much can be spent on the computers. The partner and his or her team, will then go away with a brief from all the partners with a requirement to be delivered in a given timescale. If, at the next partners' meeting, the project is behind schedule, the other partners are entitled to ask why and insist on a strict adherence to the next date. If enough fuss is made because the work was not delivered on time, it is likely that the partner in charge will make sure that next time, he or she adheres to the timetable. They may also decide that they won't volunteer next time around!

The committee must work to the business strategy with committed and enthusiastic partners. This can work in practice with people in charge of their particular area of expertise and interests. This type of decision making can also increase the motivation of the partners. It is, however, very labour intensive.

THE MANAGING PARTNER

The third model is where a managing partner is appointed with authority to make decisions on behalf of the other partners. More particularly, he or she is there to ensure that things get done. The managing partner ought not to be the senior partner. The two of them should work together, however, the senior partner's role being more of a pastoral and promotional nature. The managing partner can still delegate work to individual partners if that is appropriate, as long as due regard is taken of the "soft cost" to the practice. The "soft cost" is the cost of having the practice run by other partners on £200-plus per hour when they could be fee earning. The managing partner in medium size practices may be expected to service clients as well.

The managing partner's task is to ensure the smooth running of the office and to be responsible for keeping a tight rein on all partnership activities and to meet regularly with a management team. The management team should consist of the managing and senior partner and any individual professionals within the practice. These are usually the in-house accountant, marketing manager, the computer expert and a representative from personnel.

The advantage of the third model is that the rest of the partners can get on with the job of being lawyers, without wasting valuable time running the practice. One problem appears to be in deciding who, out of the existing partners, should be the managing partner. If the question is not resolved, the practice must resort to the first or second model with the consequential lack of management efficiency.

STAFF

If the practice has not identified a management style for the partners, it is unlikely to have a cohesive management style for the staff. It is essential these days to have proper lines of communication to ensure that everybody knows what is expected of them and more particularly where the practice is going. In a small practice this should not represent a major problem as the members of staff and the partners will probably be working in close proximity with each other.

In larger practices the staff operate in different departments – litigation, corporate, etc. The individual departments should, however, operate under the same systems as the rest of the office. There needs to be a consistency of style across the firm. This idea is expanded in Chapter 8 on marketing. Even so departments can become isolated from the firm as a whole within their various disciplines. It is for this reason that "teams" are seen as a way forward. It is essential that communications between departments are maintained.

In the first instance there must be someone responsible for the staff, who can deal with staff queries and difficulties that arise on an individual basis. Secondly there must be a staff committee, where staff matters can be aired and acted upon. The members of the committee must be elected by the staff, and chaired by the managing partner or the partner in charge of staff. That committee will deal with all matters that affect staff and will be a sounding board for new ideas and incentives. The managing partner or the partner in charge of the staff will report (as he or she considers necessary) to the partners at their meetings, matters of general concern that arise from the staff meetings. The minutes of the meetings can be taken by different members of the staff on the committee and disseminated to the rest of the office either as a formal minute, or on the intranet.

In addition to the staff meetings, which should perhaps be held on a regular basis, there should be department meetings. These are meetings of all the people involved in each department. If there are a large number of people, it may be necessary to split the group. Individual fee earners and partners might well have to meet more frequently.

TEAM MEETINGS

Meetings of the entire department are also a useful forum to disseminate information arising from partners' meetings and events of importance within the practice. It ought to be general policy to identify matters with which the partnership or other departments are pleased. For example, the satisfactory conclusion of a client matter; the introduction of a new client to the practice; matters of interest within the practice; exam successes and personal achievements, including babies! These matters are discussed in more detail in the Chapter 8.

There appears to be an unwillingness on the part of some partners to disclose figures not only to fee earners but members of staff. Some figures are sensitive (individual wages) but these can be absorbed in a general figure. It is assumed that the members of staff are considered to be an asset to the firm and to have the firm's best interests at heart. If they do not, perhaps it is worth asking why they are being employed by the practice! As a result it ought to be possible to disclose the anticipated fees; the overall salary costs; the overall overhead costs and the profit for the department. Far too often the only figures are the fees achieved by individual partners and fee earners. If it is understood that the prosperity of the firm and the staff is dependent on hitting all the targets, there is likely to be a greater ownership of the need to work as a team and develop the department.

MANAGING TEAMS

As a partner you are going to have a team of people working for you. Teams are complex and dynamic, they are unique and have an identity of their own. If they are working well teams can be innovative, solve difficult problems, make sound decisions and help to build individual skills. If they are managed badly they can be destructive.

Groups go through various stages and this process can easily be misunderstood or overlooked. The behaviour of individuals in teams differs going through the various stages. In an undeveloped team there may be an initial attempt to get on with the job, which might be unsuccessful because at that stage there is a lack of commitment. Members of the group will be weighing up each other to see how they fit in with the team and will look to the leader for support. There will be some anxiety as all the members try to work out what is expected of them and what their contribution might be.

As the team develops members will produce ideas, be defensive in some areas and competitive in others. Undoubtedly cliques will form. All the various personalities must be accommodated if the leader is to mould the team to a position where there is uniformity of purpose and flexibility. Where mutual trust and respect develop there is less need for the leader to interfere.

The size of the team is an important factor. Teams inevitably become less effective as they get larger. If the team consists of more than 15 people it is probably as well to split it up into more manageable sizes.

Innovation is frequently seen as the key to improving profits and market share. Practices are under pressure as never before in trying to keep pace with an ever changing environment. One of the great strengths of a highly effective team is its ability to be innovative and to embrace new ideas.

Creative thinking is normally done when a person is alone and feeling relaxed and secure – usually away from the workplace. Innovation, on the other hand, is more likely to take place in the workplace and most effectively when done in groups. This is specially so when there is high level of pressure around. The culture of the practice must also encourage lateral thinking. New ideas are unlikely to be produced by fee earners and staff where they feel that errors are not to be tolerated and there is a general feeling of mistrust.

It must be appreciated that teams are not the same as committees. Committees have a specific job to do and need to find answers that satisfy all the people on the committee. As a result if the answer is blue or yellow a committee usually ends up with green! The members of the committee represent different interests within the office and have to report back to their group to see if they agree with the decisions. Teams, on the other hand are set up to be successful. Everyone involved shares the same aspirations and each should be essential to the proper working of the team. Teams need to have people with different talents. Charles Handy suggests in *Inside Organizations* that:

> "a team needs, always, among its members, people who will fill these parts: the Captain, the Administrator, the Driver, who will push the task through, and the Expert, the one with the knowledge and ideas".

It is essential that individual departments operate as teams. This will ensure that everyone involved is working to the best interest of the department. It may be that work within the department would be better handled by one specific member, who may have the expertise or may produce the best margin of profit because he or she could achieve it more cheaply than the others.

Teams fail for a wide variety of reasons. Harvey Robbins and Michael Finley suggest there is no simple reason the breakdown may include:

- Private agendas and an unwillingness to change
- Hazy vision, confused goals and cluttered objectives
- Bad decision making and poor leadership
- Insufficient feed back
- Personality conflicts and lack of trust.

Clearly a balance is needed. It is important that clients who are used to working with particular partners should continue to do so. Care must be taken in recognising that clients are clients of the practice. It is therefore important that where work is required, that could more usefully be done by another member of staff, that member should do the work but under the supervision of the lead partner or fee earner so that the relationship is retained. In time the client will agree to other members of the firm acting for them, if properly handled.

MANAGING A DEPARTMENT

Managing a department and leading a team is exciting and challenging and requires a complex number of skills of which the people skills are often the most difficult to master.

- What is your leadership style?
- How good are you at communicating?
- Can you delegate effectively?
- Can you motivate individuals?
- Do you understand the team process?
- Are you a good listener?
- Can you resolve conflict?
- What are your strengths and weaknesses?

COMMUNICATION

Let us deal with communication first. The actual words we use are only a small portion of the message we are giving to another person. We communicate more powerfully by the way we say the words; our facial expression; our stance; the way we move. Of course, our timing in delivering the message can be crucial to the way it is received. To see how this works watch a skilled politician being interviewed on television. Note the interaction of the words and body language.

If you are dealing with staff, what are you intending to communicate? It is worth briefly considering what you are trying to achieve at any given time. How should you behave to get the results you want? How is the other person likely to respond? A few minutes of preparation can often prevent misunderstanding, particularly in a potentially difficult situation. Telephone and written communication require an adjustment of skills and style. The former needing words, tone and the use of silence.

The basic rule in communication is to keep it short and simple. Lengthy reports and memos often get put to one side and never read and lengthy explanations can be misunderstood.

Listening

Listening is one of the basics of communication and is critical in being effective both in and out of work, yet most people are not trained to listen. If you do not listen properly to your staff, you will not understand them and they, in turn, will not feel able to confide in you. In general people listen in order to be able to reply to what is being said, waiting to offer their experience in a similar situation.

> "I know how you feel... Let me tell you what I did when the same thing happened to me".

The emphasis immediately shifts and the original speaker is left in a void, because there has been no attempt to really understand his/her unique circumstances and feelings. We should advise people, evaluate what has been said, ask questions, and even try to interpret behaviour and motives.

We may pretend to listen, we may listen selectively, however, we seldom listen to what is actually being said and try to understand the other person's perspective. It requires a lot more effort to watch behaviour closely, pick up the feelings, note what is not said or is being skimmed over and be aware of any incongruences between words and body language. Understanding another person's position and more importantly being able to communicate that understanding, is a powerful tool. It can be used with clients, staff and even at home! Failure to communicate effectively can have a demoralising effect on staff.

Break down in communications

Communications break down for many reasons, people don't listen properly. They fail to pass on information or they withhold part of the data. They may give conflicting messages because their body language and tone of voice do not match the words that are being spoken. Perhaps they cannot present their ideas clearly, or they are domineering or aggressive.

Communication is at the core of managing individuals. In simple terms this involves setting clear objectives, reprimanding when necessary and praising people when they perform well.

OBJECTIVES

Defining objectives sounds easy enough, yet many managers fail at this first hurdle.

"Do your best" or "Just get on with it" is not the answer.

To be effective you must:

- Define objectives
- Agree standards
- Set targets.

Achieving objectives result in you and your team contributing to the practice as a whole. Standards are what you are going to be measured against by your clients and external governing bodies. These are best demonstrated by achieving industry standards such as Lexcel, Investors in People, RS 900 and the Legal Aid Franchise.

Targets are set with individuals in your team and if correctly done can be a good motivator for them. Setting personal objectives is extremely important. These need to be understandable, which means that they must be specific, measurable, realistic and time bound.

MAKING MISTAKES

Staff will make mistakes from time to time. How mistakes are dealt with in the partnership depends upon the practice culture. Where the culture deplores mistakes, staff become defensive and cover up mistakes. The result will be that less learning is achieved. In other words there will be a blame culture and no one will take any risks. This type of culture can best be seen in large organisations where bureaucracy is rife. Everybody sticks to the job they have been given and are unwilling to go out on a limb, because if they do it incorrectly they will be in trouble. It means that there is very little imagination and probably not a lot of camaraderie.

ALLOWING FOR MISTAKES

Ideally you should allow people to extend their abilities. If they get it wrong it should be looked on as a learning curve. It only becomes a problem if they keep making the same mistake.

Using this type of approach there is a potential for learning from errors, which should lead to the avoidance of similar errors in future. It is not surprising that there seems to be a correlation between superior performance and a climate that is non-blaming.

REPRIMANDING

Kenneth Blanchard and Spencer Johnson in their book entitled *The One Minute Manager* set out constructive methods of reprimanding a member of staff. They suggest that the process is split into two sections.

THE FIRST HALF

- It is important that you reprimand somebody immediately you learn of the mistake and not wait weeks or months until you do so.

- Specify what the person has done wrong. This must be explained in behavioural terms and never as a personal attack. Then it is much easier for the person to accept and they are less likely to become defensive or to blame others. Saying "I don't like your attitude" to a member of staff who has been rude to a client will not do. You have made the comment personal and will then have to explain what you mean. Far better to say "When you are speaking to clients it's not professional to lose your temper. I don't want this to happen again!"

- Tell the person how you feel about what has happened. You must be honest about it even though you may be frustrated, irritated or angry. You must say how you feel but without becoming aggressive. Stop for a few seconds. Silence is uncomfortable but it emphasises the point being made.

THE SECOND HALF

- Look the person in the eye and tell them how much you value them.
- Let them know that you appreciate how competent they usually are, that you think well of them, but not of their performance in this situation.
- Let the matter drop and do not refer to it again.

UNDER-PERFORMING

If a member of staff is under-performing you need to:

- Identify the required standard.

- Identify the gap between the person's current performance and what is required.
- Agree an action plan.
- Agree a time span for the person to achieve the required standard.
- Agree specific dates for meetings to review their progress.

PRAISING

Acknowledging that a member of staff has done something right, even something exceptional, seems to be particularly difficult for many people, including partners. The reverse seems to be true of criticism: most managers are quick to criticise and often appear to be looking for faults. Praising staff is seldom done, but people need to be noticed, they want to be valued and they need attention and recognition.

Eric Berne used the term "stroking" to describe any form of recognition from one person to another. "Strokes" are classified as positive or negative, and can be verbal or non-verbal. A verbal "stroke" can be anything from a greeting to a full conversation, whilst a non-verbal "stroke" can be a smile, nod, wave etc.

A positive "stroke" is intended to be pleasurable for the recipient, a negative stroke is unpleasant.

If you tell a trainee solicitor that he or she has done a good piece of work you have just given him or her a positive "stroke".

If you walk into your department one morning, do not smile, acknowledge the staff, as they say "Good Morning" you have delivered a negative "stroke" to everyone you have come in contact with.

A reprimand, of course, is a negative "stroke". It would be logical to think that people would always seek positive "strokes" and wherever possible avoid negative ones. Stewart and Joines maintain that any "stroke" is better than none. If there seem to be few or no positive "strokes" available, the person may set up situations in which other people will give him or her negative "strokes". This is usually done without awareness and helps to explain why people repeat behaviour that appears to be self-defeating.

"Stroking" reinforces behaviour, therefore, when behaviour has the required effect and gets the wanted "stroke" the person is likely to repeat the behaviour.

This applies to both positive and negative "strokes", since some people adopt behaviour which will get a negative response.

There is a subjective value attached to the "strokes", depending on who gives the "stroke" and the way in which it is given.

If the senior partner reprimands a member of staff and does so by raising his or her voice, the staff member is going to be more affected than if he or she is told off by a junior partner using a similar tone of voice.

MANAGEMENT CULTURE

It is against this background that a solicitor learns to manage. Very few, if any, have formal training in management or its techniques. The position between the partners could be exacerbated further because each partner has an equity stake in the business. The partners may recognise a lack of management skills in one of their number, but could be loath to allow any one partner or set of partners to have the final say as to how the practice should be run. This is particularly so if such decisions are going to affect the amount of money he or she already has in the practice, or the amount of money he or she might be able to draw during the year. Add to that a natural inclination to query and to correct everything and it is not surprising that managing a legal partnership is a difficult task.

The problem is, of course, that whether the partners like it or not they are running a business, frequently a substantial business and not a home for the bewildered! The consequence is that the practice and the partners must be profitable. If a partner is not making the required profit, steps need to be taken to address and rectify the situation.

LEXCEL AND LEGAL AID FRANCHISE

It can be difficult to get individual partners to become involved with the practice as a whole. Fortunately the market place dictates that all practices need to have "Kite Marks" be they RS900; Lexcel; Investors in People; the legal aid franchise and others. Each of these influence how the practice behaves in various ways and more importantly demonstrate to the outside world that the practice has systems which identify their expertise against which performance can be judged.

Lexcel, which is the Law Society's quality standard, requires the partnership, to adopt file management techniques across the board, which help supervision and more importantly create a uniformity of style. This enables partners, fee earners and other members of staff to pick up a file at any time, within their discipline and know exactly how matters stand.

The legal aid franchise has similar and more stringent requirements. It is possible, however, to run the two systems together which avoids a duplicity of effort.

A clear advantage of the two systems is that as the level of supervision goes up the level of client complaints should go down.

INVESTORS IN PEOPLE

Investors in People deals more with the communications within the office. It started in a similar way to the Lexcel and legal aid franchise, but has developed away from being document-led to being people-led. It is designed to ensure that everybody in the organisation knows what is expected of them. To this end it is necessary to have a strategy for the firm. Not only that, but staff and fee earners need to know what is expected of them within that framework. In addition, the system seeks to improve the working environment for the staff and fee earners and is specifically concerned to see that appropriate training is given at appropriate levels. Appraisals, which are discussed later in this chapter, are designed to ascertain the strengths and weaknesses of the individual members of staff and to identify their training needs to remove the weaknesses.

It needs to be appreciated that the requirements for the individual "Kite Marks" alter from time to time. There is no doubt, however, that those firms who choose not to adopt such schemes will lose out in the long term. Certainly firms involved with legal aid will have found that failure to obtain the franchise means that "Legal Aid Contracts" cannot be awarded to them. These firms might well take the view that the level of pay on legally aided work is such that it is not profitable in any event. As the number of firms doing legal aid drops, there is pressure on those who are left to be remunerated at a better level. This is a business decision that will be influenced by the shape of the firm and the environment in which it operates.

The downside to the "Kite Marks" is undoubtedly the "soft cost". Suppose there are 35 fee earners and partners and three of their files have to be examined each month by a supervisor, then 105 files must be checked every month. If the average check takes 20 minutes per file then 2,100 minutes or

35 hours are needed every month just to check the files. Over a year this amounts to 420 hours. If the average charge-out rate for a supervisor is £145, the "soft cost" to the firm is £60,900. That cost does not include the administrator's time in checking that the files are being reviewed properly and in Legal Aid work that the appropriate financial records are being kept so that the board can be sure that the system is working correctly.

It may well be though that implementing such schemes reduces negligence claims over a 12-month period. With premiums running at about 5%+ of turnover, excluding the liability of a practice to find the first £50,000 to £75,000 of any claims, one claim could exceed the "soft cost" in any event.

This book is about turning a practice into a business, that is making partners realise that they are not operating in isolation from each other, and more importantly of the market place. As a result business techniques that are seldom learnt by the professions are essential if the firm is to progress. In addition to the "soft costs" of "Kite Marks" there is all the additional time expended in running and promoting the business. In view of the costs involved it is sensible to adopt tried and tested systems which help in running the practice.

STAFF APPRAISALS

Appraisal schemes can be notoriously inefficient, ineffective, disruptive and often viewed with suspicion. Ian Beardwell and Les Holden suggest that an appraisal has two purposes:

- to assess performance and link it to pay awards
- to assess performance to highlight training and development needs.

You will be looking not only at the staff's current abilities but also at their potential. They go on to suggest that these two purposes should not be amalgamated into the same interview, because they require different procedures and information to implement them. For instance, if you were to use the same interview to discuss a pay rise and training needs, you would never get commitment to new objectives if the salary rise was far below the person's expectations!

There is likely to be a central wage structure with appropriate bonus or incentives built in. It would therefore be quite wrong to agree a wage increase in an appraisal which did not fit in with the central structure. The appraisal may, however, reveal skills which justify the consideration of an increase of wage when the wage reviews come round.

Further, it may not be possible to upgrade an individual's position at the appraisal. It would, however, be possible to bring such a suggestion to the attention of the appropriate body in due course.

The appraisal is basically a performance review, which is clearly the responsibility of the partner or fee earner in charge of the department. The appraisal interview is to ensure that individuals can carry out the work expected of them and can further develop their skills and performance.

The task is to set objectives and assess performance. Appraising is not easy. It is important that the individuals who are going to appraise receive some coaching so that there is uniformity of style. Although solicitors and fee earners are used to interviewing clients, that skill is not the same as the one required for an appraisal!

In reality many partners and fee earners will not enjoy appraising their staff. It seems to be a peripheral activity that gets in the way of the job, and appears to have little relevance to the running of the office. Many find it stressful, dealing with emotional matters in a "counsellor" role, does not sit easily with solicitors in general. Dealing with either end of the performance continuum – high flyers and poor performers – is relatively easy. It is much more difficult to deal with the majority of staff who fall in the middle. Some members of staff reached a level of competence and do not anticipate developing much further. More of the same is not necessarily defeatist if an individual is fulfilling a proper function and has no higher aspirations.

Although there may be a formal appraisal once a year, the activity should really be continuous – albeit without paperwork and on an informal basis.

Assessing performance is not easy. Some organisations use a rating scale in their performance reviews. However, these can be very subjective across a range of appraisers, which may make it difficult to compare results on a meaningful basis. Further a rating scale does not help when deciding how to develop the individual's performance.

The appraisal interview should be about you discussing various incidents with the member of staff; reviewing what did or did not happen; and discussing how a similar situation could be dealt with in future. You need to collect information and to do this you need to ask questions, and **listen** properly to the answers. You must be careful that you do not ask leading questions! The questions should be open, such as "What happened? How could you have prevented it?" You will be surprised what comes out if a member of staff feels reasonably comfortable and realises that for once you have time to listen to them!

At the end of the appraisal you must get the person to agree to a future course of action. It is worth remembering that, if the individual comes up with the ideas, there is far more likelihood that they will implemented. If you want somebody to change, you need their agreement and commitment rather than their compliance with your ideas. If all you achieve is a resigned agreement to comply with your wishes, you can expect non-compliance down the track.

There are many forms of appraisal system and it is necessary for you to tailor one or more of them to suit your office. They are very difficult to do well but undoubtedly against a background of a caring environment they can be immensely helpful. It is worth bearing in mind that appraisals can be a double-edged sword. If you have dealt with appraisals in a fairly offhand way and generally confirmed that the member of staff is performing satisfactorily, you might find that were you to ask them to leave because they are not performing, that might be difficult to sustain in the light of the appraisal.

PARTNER APPRAISAL

There are firms which have introduced partner appraisal who wished that they had not. This does not mean that appraisals should not be attempted, but great care needs to be taken. The purpose of the appraisal is to identify not only the partner's strengths and weaknesses, but also to see how that individual partner's contribution to the practice as a whole can be improved. It is important that the method used to attain that end is uniform for all partners.

The effect of the appraisal should be to make partners more accountable to their colleagues and for them to create a strategy for their contribution to the practice. A consequence of the appraisals must therefore be that each partner maps out his or her training requirements for the coming year.

If staff appraisals are difficult, partner appraisals are very difficult. This book is an attempt to make partners realise that they are running a business. That means the business needs to make an adequate profit to satisfy the aspirations of the partnership. It also needs to know how the market place is changing and what should be done about it. In those circumstances it is inevitable that from time to time partners get out of step with the needs of the practice. If a partner or partners are performing well it would be helpful to find out why, so that others can follow suit. There is after all no point in re-inventing the wheel.

If on the other hand a partner or partners are underperforming, it is sensible to find out what the problems are and what might be done about it. Experience shows that difficulties need to be tackled sooner rather than later. They rarely go away and frequently become far more complex.

If you can manage a partnership you can manage anything. There are very few commercial organisations where the ownership and management are so intrinsically mixed together. As a result a group of partners can influence the way the practice behaves even though this might not be commercially sound.

It is clear from the above that partner appraisals need to be approached with considerable caution. Partner appraisals run the risk of either massaging existing egos, or castigating partners who are underperforming. Both stances are unacceptable. The object of the exercise is to ascertain whether the partners are doing the job effectively. If they are, what further help do they need to improve and expand their abilities? If they are not, what can be done about it? Ultimately this could include asking a partner to leave the practice if nothing can be done and matters are only getting worse.

CONCLUSION

It may well be that your perception is that the management of the practice is not too bad. The figures are being maintained. There may be a slight increase in the staff costs but that is to be expected. You are carrying out appraisals. It is true that not much attention is being paid to them, and you suspect that the staff will please themselves whatever you do. Some are demotivated and, of course, there are on-going personality clashes! Team meetings have been postponed rather too regularly, but the actual work has to be done, and all the partners seem busy.

However, as Harvey-Jones pointed out, standing still is not an option in business. You can rest assured that someone down the road is already quietly taking clients from you. Unfortunately it takes some time for mismanagement to become obvious and by then the culture is well entrenched. It is therefore doubly hard to get out of the rut. Most of us only take notice when we are hurting. In partnerships that tends to be when margins are getting tighter and less money is available for drawings. In addition the capital accounts start to go down!

It is not universally accepted that taking care of staff, being careful with your clients and acting with integrity will produce the desired result. We all know for ourselves, however, that the occasional "thank you" and individual concern for our well-being goes a long way. We all like to be recognised as being of some value, why should our staff, colleagues and clients be any different? In the long term there is no doubt that a happy ship is a productive ship. It is unfortunate that most of us have not had the opportunity to learn the skills that make it so. Perhaps it is time we learned before it is too late.

How are you doing? Questions in relation to your practice and departments

1. Do you have a partnership deed?
2. Who manages the practice?
3. Is this satisfactory?
4. What are your leadership styles?
5. Are your teams working well?
6. If not why not?
7. Have you an appraisal system?
8. Does the appraisal system include partners?

CHAPTER 7
STRATEGIC PLANNING

"We have some very competent lawyers. The clients know it and we really don't need to worry about where our work is going to come from."

THE BACKGROUND

If getting the budget organised was difficult, then attempting to decide where the practice is going in the long term is going to be even more so. The same management problems apply to running the practice as a whole. Many of the partners are often not business minded. They are so tied up with their work that they cannot recognise that it has a pattern. It is either growing, static, or declining. The reason that this is not recognised is that, until recently, solicitors have been very fortunate, their market place really only started to become susceptible to change in the late 1980s and early 1990s. This was principally brought about by the recession. In the past, middle of the road provincial and smaller city practices had relied on a staple diet of conveyancing, probate, and some litigation. Litigation was really the poor relation to the rest of the practice and was often only tolerated because it enabled firms to service the litigious needs of local wealthy families.

Much of the turnover in these small practices was property related; mainly domestic, but also with some commercial work. The recession reduced the amount of work available in the marketplace. As a result solicitors attempted to boost their share of the market by reducing their fees. This was something that would have been unheard of several years previously. Clients began to realise that, not only was there a shortage of work, but they could shop around for the lowest price. The problem was that many other practices were having to do the same. As much of the profession was unaware of net margins and profitability and indeed on the way the marketplace operated, they assumed that increased volume (driven by lower prices) would solve the problem and bring turnover back to healthier levels. Unfortunately it did not.

Clients were used to shopping around and the fees for routine work became ridiculously low. Enter the licensed conveyancers, who were prepared to work for a much lower profit than solicitors were used to. They could, therefore, undercut the solicitors by even more, to the delight of the domestic client.

When licensed conveyancers looked at the possibility of setting up on their own, they discovered that it was a lot more expensive than they had at first realised. As a result many solicitors took them into their practices to run their conveyancing departments.

While all this was going on, and to make matters worse, computers had advanced beyond all recognition. There were dedicated event-driven systems on the market that would "do" conveyancing for you. The more astute solicitors either used the systems or wrote bespoke systems for themselves. Either way it meant that even less qualified staff could, in conjunction with licensed conveyancers, carry out large volumes of work at costs which allowed for a reasonable margin.

Unfortunately solicitors no longer controlled the housing marketplace. Banks and building societies discovered that they could carry out conveyancing transactions, also using licensed conveyancers, or better still disenchanted solicitors. Further, the funding available to them and their national networks enabled them to generate huge numbers of house sales and remortgaging opportunities. They could afford to go to large firms of solicitors (who by this time were anxious to achieve a high volume) and strike deals with which no one else could compete. As a by-product they also locked the solicitors into their organisation because they could not afford to see the volume disappear. After all, if solicitors were achieving say 400 remortgages a month at a cost to the client of £90, they generated £36,000 per month and £432,000 per annum. If their margins were 25%, that is £108,000 net. That is more than some smaller practices were making in the good times. Of course, the firms needed to gear up their offices both by the increased use of computers and the employment of less qualified staff.

The question is, ought those firms who relied to a large extent on conveyancing have been aware that this scenario would occur? The answer must be yes. If they did not understand how conveyancing worked better than outsiders, they really should not have been in the business in the first place! Once clients realized that not only were solicitors' fees negotiable but that other firms would also compete for the business, they were able to apply the same principles to other areas of legal work – personal injury work, legal aid, the formation of companies, etc. It is essential that the profession learns from its mistakes and takes a serious look at the particular marketplace.

THE SOLUTION

You must know where you are going. Sir John Harvey-Jones says that the most dangerous situation is when businesses are not going anywhere at all. A strategic plan gives you direction. How do you go about preparing a strategic plan? Strategic planning can be broken down into several areas.

First, you need to establish your current position and where trends are likely to take it. Look at your competitors and then consider a wider environment.

Second, produce a long term plan. It is difficult to identify where the practice might be in seven or eight years from now. It is clear, however, that unless there is a general understanding as to what its shape may be in that sort of timescale, the firm will lack a general direction. For example does it see itself expanding by acquisition or internal growth or not expanding at all? Does it see itself becoming a specialist practice? Whatever is decided will dictate the shape of the firm and more particularly the structure of the long-term plan.

The third plan is for the medium term. The three-to-five year plan can be much more specific, but is set against the background of where the partners see the practice going ultimately. The medium term plan actually states what the expectations of the practice and its individual departments are going to be.

The fourth area is the short term plan. If you have prepared a budget and forecast, this is the short term plan. It is likely these days that most firms will have had a budget and forecast and that is the best place to start.

ANALYSING

First, as always, you must convince all the partners that this is something which has to be done. As a budget and forecast has been prepared it might make sense to ask the in-house accountant or the firm's accountants to prepare a statement showing turnover over the previous five years. This will reveal what growth there has been. The turnover should then be broken down to reveal the increase or otherwise in the various departments, which make up the practice. The figures should then show what the actual costs of the running each department are over the same periods. These figures consist of the actual wages in each department; the budgeted costs for advertising and marketing, library, training, and temporary staff; and the fixed overhead costs pro-rated to individual departments by reference to the number of people working in each department.

The resulting figures are the net profit for each department over the five-year period. As each partner will be involved in a department, appropriate notional salaries for the partners must be deducted to reveal the true profit in each department.

It is quite likely that these figures will produce results that were not expected. They might reveal that, although the partners thought they ran a predominantly litigious practice, in fact they have made the bulk of their profits in their probate department! If the figures also show the number of jobs completed in each department over the same period, it may be possible to ascertain whether a department is growing or shrinking. It is obviously essential to know if the figures are going up or down and if so their relationship to the fees generated.

Armed with the above information a meeting of the partners can be called so that they can see where they are and where they have come from. The figures are likely to be dramatic enough to persuade them that they cannot allow another five years to pass without giving some thought to the likely shape of the practice. It is absolutely certain that if they do nothing the business will still have a shape, but that shape will not necessarily be the one they want. If they wish to influence where the partnership is going they need to sit down and decide what they want.

PUTTING PLANS IN HAND

It is unlikely that the partners would want to include any fee earners in the initial discussion. However, the overall plan must work "top-down" and "bottom-up". Initially it may be enough to work "top-down" by getting the partners together to discuss the figures, the starting position and the five year plan. This is best achieved by arranging an 'away day' where the matter in hand can be properly thought about without interminable interruptions from telephones and staff. Getting all the partners away together is no mean feat, but it can be achieved if there is the will to do it and hopefully the historical view of the practice will have persuaded the partners that they must do something about it. What is absolutely certain is that if thought is not given to where the practice is going it is very unlikely to achieve any of the aspirations that individual partners might have, but have not articulated.

In addition to getting the partners away from the office it makes sense, on the first occasion, to have a facilitator. It is difficult enough to get some consensus from partners, in any event, but if you are relying on one of the partners to lead, it is unlikely that he or she will have sufficient credibility to motivate the others. An outsider can say all the things that partners would like to say but may not be able to without giving offence. He or she can also attack "sacred cows" – "It's been good enough for me for the last 20 years and I haven't done too badly" may or may not be right, but it is singularly unhelpful.

STAGE 1

It is necessary to consider the strengths and weakness of all the departments. The marketplace will be different for each department. It consists not only of other solicitors and their firms but also any other businesses, banks, building societies, insurance companies, estate agents, etc. who might be seeking to provide the same service as you to their customers. In addition, the firm's marketplace does not necessarily work in a vacuum and might well be influenced by political pressures both local and national. If for example a large housing development is to be build out of town, how will that impact on your practice, or more importantly on your clients. Might some fundamental legislation, the Human Rights Act 1998 for example, have a fundamental effect on the practice?

Although the partners may not wish to include fee earners in their first 'away day', they may feel, that there should be some dialogue with them within the department to see how they perceive the department developing and what threats or opportunities might exist. If it is possible to have that sort of discussion at this stage, even though it might not be very well focused, such views clearly are valuable at the strategic meeting itself. The strategic meetings should in the longer term involve the fee earners, because in that way they will own the strategy and therefore see that it is achieved.

The examination by departments of the historical background, the strengths and weaknesses in each department and perceived threats and opportunities, does not end there. You have to work with existing staff, buildings, clients and your current image (whatever that might be). You may not know what your image is. It is perfectly feasible to ask a market research agency to carry out some research for you.

It is also sensible to look at the various surveys which affect your kind of business. Reference has already been made to the surveys by PriceWaterhouseCooper and there are many others.

STAGE 2

It will be clear that a great deal of work has to be done before the partners (and fee earners) can sit down and decide on a way forward. The problem is that some partners are so busy doing the work that they cannot find time to carry out the appropriate research. They complain that the "soft time" is enormous.

If the cost of all the partners, at partner rate and the fees of the facilitator are added together they represent a very large slice of the turnover. Those partners might suggest that, if the strategy meetings were to be abandoned, the firm could get on with earning money and the extra profit would be greater than the potential earning achieved from the exercise. That view would be very short sighted because all markets, including the legal marketplace, are changing substantially. Partners cannot afford to be complacent about where their market is going. They must face up to the possibility that some of them may have no work in five years time! Many a company has gone out of business this way.

The information obtained from the budget, the consideration of the market place and general thoughts on where each department might be going is a vital framework against which the strategic direction can be planned. It is perhaps as well to remember Alfredo Pareto's famous 80/20 rule. This identifies that 80% of a firm's revenue is usually generated by 20% of the clients. It therefore makes sense to examine first the 20% of the clients who are generating that business to see if they can provide additional work. It is after all much easier to generate extra work from existing clients, than to try to create new work from new clients. Any attempt to obtain a new client will normally have a gestation period of 18 months to two years and in many cases a lot longer. This is discussed in more detail in Chapter 8 on marketing.

The figures will also have revealed those departments which are making very little profit and those that are making losses. Applying Pareto's rule, there is little point in spending a lot of time in these areas other than to decide whether they are to be kept on or closed down. The areas to concentrate on are those showing the best margins. These are the areas where you need to decide their position in the business cycle. Do they represent growth areas, or are they in decline? If the latter, what is the likely timescale of their demise and what are you going to do about it? It is also worth observing that 80% of what is achieved comes from 20% of the effort. This rather begs the question that, if you could increase the effort even by ten per cent, then presumably the profit might increase also. It would make sense to examine the various activities of the partners. If full time sheets are being maintained it ought to be possible to identify what the partners do with their time. It is likely that they spend more time doing the things they enjoy. It might be, however, that writing articles, attending charitable organisations, or being involved with other organisations such as local or national law societies are a lot of fun but make little contribution to the firm. Unless these activities can be justified either financially or from a marketing point of view it might make sense to stop doing them.

The strategy has to be a living document. The decisions must be specific, measurable, achievable, realistic and time bound (SMART). It is perhaps sensible to have headings that cover all the departments so that there is some uniformity of approach. These could cover such things as:

- the marketplace you are operating in
- the services you provide
- the people or staff you need in each department and the office as a whole to provide those services
- the likely profit
- the facilities in the form of buildings IT etc.
- the clients and how they are to be serviced.

The strategy will identify the timescale against which individual targets will operate and identify who will be responsible for carrying out the proposals.

Mission statements

A fundamental part of the strategy must be the mission statement. There appears to be a lot of misunderstanding about mission statements. They are designed to encapsulate in a few sentences what the business stands for. They ought to highlight how firms are different from one another. Given that solicitors business are to a large extent the same, however, this is not always easy to achieve.

The mission statement needs to be straightforward because it should be the yardstick against which actions within the practice are benchmarked. The mission statement must be succinct if it is to be memorized by all the partners, fee earners and staff. Furthermore it needs to be intelligible. Many mission statements look as if they have been drafted by consultants with very little understanding about the workings of a law practice.

The mission statement has to be seen and understood by all staff, and therefore must appear on the walls in all rooms. It is essential that the ideas contained in it are fully embraced by the whole practice. This is, after all, part of the ethos of Investors in People.

The first thing to do is to set goals within the general framework.

Goals: The likely profit

This goal might be to generate the highest net profit for the partners compatible with a good working environment. This sentiment would have to tie in with the general philosophy for the firm. It would not do for a firm to want to be the best corporate firm in the country, if this in turn required the partners and fee earners to work 1,800 productive hours a year including most weekends and holidays!

Having settled on a goal you then need to set out how you are going to achieve it. Staying with the highest profit compatible with a good working environment the objective could be achieved by agreeing the percentage of the net profit. If the average net profit for the smaller practice is 25%, the firm could attempt to ensure that each department is so organised that it produces at least a 25% profit on a sufficiently high turnover. It might therefore be better to couple the 25% net profit figure with an actual share of profit, i.e. a minimum of £75,000 per partner.

Goals: The services you will provide

Not every department may be able to achieve 25%. For example the commercial department should be able to achieve substantially more than that. Private client work may struggle to break even. In those circumstances it needs to be decided whether to continue providing such work. That decision should depend on the perception within the firm of whether clients from other departments need the assistance of that department. The practice might be loath to allow their clients to go to another practice who might inevitably pick up commercial work from those clients. Commercial judgement is required. It would not be necessary to take drastic action unless the department was actually not achieving break even. This would of necessity mean that the profit for the rest of the firm was being diluted by that department (although it must be recognised that it is still making a contribution to overhead costs). There is bound to be a time when the other partners take the view that the position is unsustainable. At least if the matter has been discussed and thought about, a proper decision for everybody involved can be made.

Action plans

Having set the goals for the strategy it is then necessary to decide on an action plan. Each department must be considered under each goal. For example, if the personal injury department is being considered it will be necessary to consider the audit by the accountants. Supposing that shows that the number of jobs is falling but the department is still achieving a net profit of say 20%. The partners need to consider the strengths, weakness, opportunities and threats as they affect the department. It may be that the department has partners and fee earners with a wide range of skills. The firm may well have an on-going level of work with a good client base. The weaknesses may be that the department lacks direction as a whole. Partners and fee earners are not prepared to give up work to each other even though others are more experienced or less costly. The object of the exercise is, after all, to get the net profit up to 25%. The department may feel that there are considerable opportunities open to them. If the practice is a legal aid practice which has the franchise and the appropriate contracts, they may feel these are worth pursuing because they can get the volume up, even though the fees are low.

If the practice is entering into the No Win – No Fee market, there may be the cash consequence mentioned earlier. If the firm currently handles 1,200 cases and the average spend by the practice to run the action on a no win no fee basis is £500 and if none of the matters settle within say nine months, there will be a requirement to fund £600,000. In an existing practice there may already be £250,000 of funding. An increase of a further £350,000 would however be considerable. If it is estimated that the no win no fee scenario will actually increase billings by say 20% or more, then once the fees start coming in the overdraft requirement could reduce. A judgement needs to be made with a contingency plan if things do not work out as expected. For more on this, see *No Win No Fee*, Kerry Underwood, details on page 164.

STAGE 3

The partners would also have to take a view as to what might happen in the next three to five years. The effect of computers and more particularly the internet need to be considered. It would also make sense to ask the accountants to produce a model of the likely fee structure over the next three to five years to see what the actual effect of the increased funding and fees might be. It would then be possible to set out a timetable of the likely events. There might well be an IT implication to be worked into the strategy. There would certainly be a marketing requirement to ensure that the firm has a high enough profile to attract the work. Given that most others would be operating on a similar basis it is essential that the firm offers something which is different from the rest.

The strategy will then identify the objects for the department and the action plan to achieve those objectives. Against each part of the action plan will appear the name or names of the individuals who are charged with doing specific work, coupled with a date by when tasks must be completed. Again the actions needed to be specific, measurable, achievable, and time bound. They should also be kept as simple as possible.

The rest of the strategy will be built up in the same way. At the end of the session, which might well run into more than the one day, it should be possible to produce a written strategy for the next three to five years, identifying what is to be done, who is to do it, and by what date. Like the budget and forecast, however, it is necessary to return to the strategy, quarterly or half-yearly, to see if it is being achieved. If it is not then it will be necessary to go back to the drawing board and consider all the options.

It is unlikely that a strategy will be achieved the first time around. It may be that lip service is paid to it because one of the "kite marks" (the legal aid franchise or Investors in People) require a strategy. As the marketplace and more particularly those organisations who perceive solicitors' work to be lucrative move into the law, however, it is absolutely essential to know where you are going and how you are going to get there. If you do not the world will pass you by.

If you do not hold strategic meetings, how do you know that you are going in the right direction? You may be heading the wrong way. Worse still you may be going nowhere at all. It is all too easy to keep busy, keep your head down, and maintain the status quo, only to find that you have been left behind by your competitors.

Once you have a strategic direction the challenge is to put the plan into action. To do this you need commitment from the staff. They need to understand what you are trying to achieve, so it is very important that you share the ideas and listen to their feed-back, until everybody has ownership of the goals and believes them to be realistic and achievable.

How are you doing? Questions in relation to your practice and departments

1. Do you know what sort of practice you are in?
2. If so are all the areas within which you operate viable in the longer term?
3. If not what should you be doing about it?
4. What is the competition doing?
5. What are the less obvious competition doing? (Other professionals, the banks, building societies and insurance companies?)
6. Have you had a strategic meeting and if so have you included the fee earners and senior staff?

CHAPTER 8
MARKETING

"I work for Bowles Green and Howes Solicitors" "What are they like?" "Terrible!"

Marketing a solicitor's practice is no different from marketing any other business. The purpose is to find out what the client in each discipline wants and then to ensure that the organisation delivers that service at a reasonable price and profit.

Marketing is not only about selling and advertising, in fact advertising has only small part to play. Marketing combines all facets of the promotional mix. It relates to everything that the partners, fee earners and staff do to ensure that a consistent message is given to the public. It is essential that the firm understands the message it wishes to get across to the marketplace in general and that it ensures that all the internal functions that interface with the client, are presented to their best advantage. Only when the firm knows where it is going, what services it wishes to deliver and at what level, is there any point in it going out to the marketplace to sell its wares.

Many practices have not thought out a proper business strategy. They have had meetings to discuss where the firm is, in general terms. They have made some attempt to decide where it is going, but they have not "bought in" to the idea that, unless there is a seriously structured strategy identifying exactly what the plan and the priorities are, the firm will drift. The drift might be generally in the right direction but will not be focused enough to produce the desired results.

The purpose of the marketing activity is to promote the marketing priorities derived from the strategic plan. If there is no proper strategy how can there be a proper marketing strategy? Most practices have a "marketing budget" but quite often do not have a proper marketing strategy which will justify the spending of the money. As much of the "Marketing effort" seems to revolve round advertising, often without any provision for monitoring the results, there must be large sums of money being spent possibly to very little advantage. The position is further complicated by individual departments clinging on to their marketing spend, as agreed in the budget, because they do not want to lose it, rather than realising that the money could be better spent elsewhere in the business.

Assuming that there is a business strategy, it is likely that the firm will be looking to promote amongst other things:

- that it has expertise
- that it is caring
- that it has integrity
- that it works to a very high standard.

Whatever the list might be, you can rest assured that the competition has exactly the same list and that these are all "givens". The problem the firm has is to show why it is different to the competition.

INTERNAL ORGANISATION

It is essential that the firm ensures that its internal systems are in place before it goes out to the public and its clients to say what it does and how it does it. For example, it is rather like a manufacturing company advertising its product for sale before it has installed the machinery to make it and tested that it is working properly. After all, it is unproductive to spend even a modest amount of money promoting a firm if there is nobody properly trained to handle the in-coming requests to ensure that contacts are converted to clients. This would not be dissimilar to having the best sports team in the world but with no player who could actually score the goals or tries! All the effort from the rest of the team would have been wasted.

STAFF

Chapter 6 indicated what can happen if the systems in the office are not effective enough when handling staff. Everybody in the office should be an ambassador for the firm. It is counter-productive to have disgruntled staff who go round telling everybody what poor employers you are. It is important that all the staff wish to encourage friends, relations and neighbours to use the practice. They should also have any such introduction properly acknowledged.

PREMISES

The firm must decide on the visual image it wishes to display. In this context the partners must recognise that there is a minimum standard that the public now expects for the fabric of the office, the reception area, and the way in which staff and others address them. They also expect the office to have the latest technology. As a result it is essential that the firm checks on how their building appears to others and how their clients are handled when they arrive to instruct the firm. The first impressions will indicate to the client whether you can actually deliver all those attributes which they consider to be "givens". Remember you do not get a second chance at a first impression: the client just goes elsewhere!

TELEPHONE AND RECEPTION

Is the telephone answered efficiently and courteously? Have you tried ringing in, incognito, to see what sort of reception you get? Can the person you are talking to give the desired advice? Is the reception area pleasant and, more importantly, is it possible for the client to indicate, not only who he or she wishes to see, but what they are seeing them about, in a confidential environment? It is unlikely that the clients will want to disclose confidential information to a room full of people. Will they be gratified to note from the magazines that the Titanic has sunk? An impression of the practice will be gleaned as soon as a client contacts the firm or comes into the offices.

STYLE

If the practice is looking to carry out substantial commercial work, it will need to look prosperous and extremely efficient. Commercial clients expect an efficient and technically advanced environment; after all that is how many of them run their own businesses. If the firm is running a legal criminal aid practice it must look clean and efficient but need not necessarily look expensive. The design and colour schemes will depend upon the type of clientele and the image the firm wishes to portray.

The matter does not end there. There should be a common "house style" for all documentation. After all, if you are trying to increase awareness of the practice, that means presenting the public with the same image and style across the board. Individual typists may want to use different typing fonts, but if a uniformity of style is required that cannot be allowed. After all if the style is not uniform the general public will get mixed messages.

MARKETING PRIORITIES

If research is carried out as to the type of work in the business and where it comes from, it is likely that over 75% consists of repeat work, recommendations from those people for whom you have acted for before and professional connections. The remaining 25% comes from new clients. It would therefore make sense to concentrate the main marketing effort on existing groups rather than on new clients. This does not mean you should not try to acquire new clients. It is an essential part of any business strategy that provisions should be made for new clients.

CROSS-SELLING

If it is accepted that over 75% of the work comes from repeat business and recommendations, it is important that the individual departments are aware of what the other departments can provide. Cross-selling means that each department advises the other departments of potential work that they could do for the client. For example, if a client is discussing his divorce and it becomes clear that he runs a successful business, the Commercial Department should be alerted to this, so that a partner or fee earner from that department can be introduced to the client. For it is likely that the client will need some advice regarding the value or structure of his business. As a result, those other departments can actively seek ways in which any existing client or recommendation can be passed on to the right person. This means that the partners and fee earners must realise that clients are clients of the firm and do not "belong" to individuals. If people pass on a client that might well affect their own targets. The firm needs to find a way to address that problem, otherwise cross-selling will not happen.

As has already been indicated, it is important that the departments working in teams are aware, from the secretaries upwards, what the firm is trying to achieve and what the expectations of the partners of the staff are. This is easier said than done. There must be regular communications up and down the organisation to ensure that everybody understands what they all do and where they are going. For example, individual departments should nominate one of their number to be responsible for disseminating information about the department to the other departments and vice versa. It might make sense for each department to provide a presentation to the other departments identifying what they and the individuals in the department do. It is not surprising that individual departments do not know what their colleagues do, if they spend the bulk of their working day dealing with client matters. They probably have little time or opportunity to know what is going on in the rest of the office. In some circumstances they may not even care.

Once each department knows what the other departments are doing it becomes slightly easier to cross-sell. Those firms that have financial service departments need an introduction to clients as soon as possible, so that a contact can be made for the potential of investment work. The trouble is that each department sees its work differently. In the litigation department the job is finished when the damages are received and the fees paid. But that is the time at which the financial services department starts. There is little point in telling the financial services department that there is an investment potential as the damages are received. Clients are far too sophisticated and the financial service market far too bullish for the client not to have sought advice at a much earlier stage. After all the client will have been given a fairly good idea of what their expectations might be at the start of the case and will in some cases already have decided how he or she are going to invest or spend the damages.

MARKETING INFORMATION

It is essential that the firm should have a standard file check list to gather key marketing information. As a minimum the list should have the client's names, date of birth, address, telephone number and details of work that the practice has done for them in the past, and a general comment as to potential work that might be required.

DATABASES

It is axiomatic that no proper marketing can be achieved without a proper database. Given the present state of the technology it ought to be simple enough to create a database at the stroke of a computer key. Unfortunately, although many computer systems do have database facilities, they are generally not properly configured and will not allow the firm to access the information in a meaningful way. As a direct result, databases do not exist in many solicitors' practices: the partners are waiting for an update on their software to allow one to be created. As it is unlikely that the partners have actually thought about how a database is to be structured, it is probably fair to say that the database will never happen! Rather than wait until a database becomes essential, it would make sense to start a new one now.

CLIENT SURVEYS AND MEETINGS

Many solicitors fail to take the obvious step and ask the clients what they would like. From time to time a client questionnaire should be sent out asking the client about the delivery of the service, what improvements they would like to see, whether the pricing structure is right and what other work they might like you to do. Many people are tempted by "freebies": perhaps the questionnaires should provide for "a draw" the winning questionnaire receiving a prize of some sort.

In the larger commercial departments, where corporate clients are involved, it would also make sense to arrange a meeting with the client to see if you are supplying appropriate service. Solicitors are diffident about this sort of approach, presumably because they might hear things that they do not want to hear. If that is the case they will find out eventually when the client ceases to instruct them! One large company actually gives a prize to the department that has the most complaints! On the face of it this seems absurd. What the company had decided, however, was that by giving a prize it would encourage the departments to discover what the complaints were so that the deficiencies could be corrected. It very quickly found that its level of complaints fell.

All the above merely accentuates that firms must handle matters efficiently in-house. They must ensure as far as possible that they gets things right from the beginning, for in that way they are more likely to satisfy their clients. The implementation of Lexcel, Investors in People and other standards will create the framework to ensure that a high standard of presentation and competency is achieved.

PRICE-DRIVEN OR BENEFIT-DRIVEN?

Marketing strategies differ depending on the perception the client has of the type of service they are expecting. At one end of the scale are the services that sell only on price. In those circumstances the marketing is wholly dependent on the pricing structure, with clients likely to choose the most competitive price for the work.

At the other extreme the clients need work undertaken because they perceive that you can obtain them a benefit, not paying a fine, saving tax, successfully acquiring the new business, etc. In those circumstances clients will want to know not only that you know the law but that you can use it to their best advantage. The price then becomes secondary. It never is totally secondary, of course, as the client will have a fairly good idea of the figure he or she considers reasonable in the marketplace generally.

The marketing requirements for the two models are quite different. "Price-driven" services may be conveyancing, wills, insolvency, simple contracts, etc. "Benefit-driven" services include commercial work, flotations, mergers and acquisitions, corporate finance, international work, estate planning, probate and trusts, tax planning and litigation. It is therefore important when deciding on the marketing mix to be aware of the type of service which is being promoted.

MARKETING OBJECTIVES

It should be clear from what has been said so far that the firm must set some marketing objectives. It must, however, ensure that it is equipped to deal with the clients from the moment they first contact the firm, up to the time that the work is completed. It must therefore have, as it first objectives, a common house style and common house procedures. It must also ensure that sufficient information is available across the practice for everybody to understand where they are going and what is expected of them.

The practice cannot do everything at once, nor should it attempt to do so. It needs to examine the type of work it is doing and develop the areas which are showing the best return. As indicated elsewhere the 80/20 rule applies. It is important that you assess which of your clients are producing the most fees. Do you know who they are and what are you going to do to keep them? It might be attractive to look to market a section of the office which is really focused, financial services for example. Whether that should be promoted will depend on the likely return. What is the margin? If the overall office margin is 25% and financial services are producing 10%, it means that the marketing spend will not be promoting an area of the business that will create the most profit.

In deciding which of the products/services to market, attention must also be paid to those services which are on the decline, and those which are beginning to grow. It may well be important to promote growing services, not because there will be an immediate return but because it is perceived that later on the firm will be much more dependent on that service than some of its current ones.

Many of the in-house arrangements will be costly in time but not in financial terms. Time spent considering the various areas of work and their contribution to the practice is valuable if it results in a proper marketing strategy based on the business strategy. Properly orchestrated, the time spent will ease the way into the promotion of the office as a whole and certain departments in particular.

PROMOTIONAL ACTIVITIES

Once the general strategy has been agreed, all the promotional activity will revolve around those concepts. It is essential that whatever device is used is monitored. If not, it is impossible to know whether it is doing you any good. As the apocryphal comment goes:

> "We know that only 50% of our marketing budget works, but we don't know which 50% !"

All, or any, of the following devices can be use for the firm as a whole, or for departments individually. Which ones you use will depend on the promotion you have in mind. Some will be more productive than others. Some may work well in one department, but not so well in another. Also realise that an idea might actually be right, but not have worked because it was not properly executed. For example, a seminar which failed to get the attendance you wanted because the home football team arrived home victoriously on the same night!

BROCHURES

Brochures have in the past been very popular with the partners, but unless they are used for a specific purpose, they can be expensive and not specially helpful. Most clients cannot be bothered to read all about the practice, particularly where many of the brochures are written for the partners rather than the clients. Perhaps the same end could be achieved by providing the client with a folder, which contains general details about the firm, with the opportunity not only to provide the client with meaningful information with regard to the work in hand, but also somewhere to keep relevant letters and papers. The folder would, of course, be in the house colours and in house type style.

ARTICLES

Local and national papers are always happy to receive copy on matters of interest. There is usually enough going on externally and within your office for something to appear at least once a week. If you can take photographs, the press are often glad to use them. Many papers will go further and have a selection of photographs of partners and others which they can use as and when they need to. It pays to know the person (agency) who will actually be involved in placing the article in the appropriate paper. A lunch (see below) with the individual will pay handsomely and keep you in touch with the paper. It is worth remembering that people move on and you need to know who the next contact will be. If you have an in-house marketing manager, it will be his or her responsibility to keep such contacts going.

Articles should also appear in the more esoteric magazines, if there are partners or fee earners with the expertise to exploit them. You should also retain the articles in reception for clients to see. Further, the staff should know that the article is going in so that if a client mentions it, or indeed instructs the practice on the strength of it, you will be aware of this. The articles could be kept and in time might be useful in getting together a small booklet on the subject covered or in a newsletter. They could also be sent out to individual clients as a matter of interest.

RADIO

If there is a local radio station it might be useful to see if there is a programme in which the firm could become involved. It would be important, as with all marketing activity, to monitor the results of such efforts. If the number of clients created, or new business generated from existing clients produces less fees that the soft cost of providing the service (presumably free), there would be little point in continuing the activity.

NEWSLETTERS

There are proprietary organisations that will produce a newsletter for you. These are more "personal" if produced in-house, however. The difficulty is finding the time to do them properly. After all they must go out regularly, say quarterly and be accurate. In time most practices, as they get larger, will have to employ a full time marketing manager. If the practice cannot afford that luxury, a partner or fee earner will have to deal with it. The newsletter need not be long. It is unlikely that the clients will rely on it for advice. What it is intended to do is to keep your name in the forefront. It is quite likely that your clients receive newsletters from other firms. It is important therefore that they have an opportunity to read about your practice. If new staff are appointed, indicate their expertise and why they have been appointed, if a partner is retiring it would be helpful to say who the contact should for the clients who have done business with him or her. We are all interested in local gossip and clients are no different, so long as it is not a breach of confidence or scurrilous!

MAIL SHOTS

Mail shots can be very effective. As mentioned earlier, however, partners must not be disappointed with the fairly low return; a 2.5% response is quite acceptable. If it is followed up with a telephone call, the return can double to 5%. For a mail shot to work it must be focused.

The first paragraph should immediately catch the reader's attention, either by identifying a benefit or by inducing anxiety. The next paragraph should identify the firm and the person dealing with the matter together with his or her credentials. In an attempt to encourage some action, it then needs to offer some sort of "freebie". Free half hours of advice, a legal audit, etc. The letter should finish by explaining what needs to be done and should be signed by two individuals, who should include their business cards. The letter should not exceed one side of A4 and needs to be written in a style which the client appreciates and not legal jargon!

If the firm has in-house leaflets or books which are relevant to the subject matter of the mail shot, they should be offered to anyone who responds. Once there has been a response it is essential that it is dealt with immediately. It is no use leaving it to the following week. It is amazing how quickly people lose interest. If clients are achieved in this way they need to go on the database and a record of the number of "hits" for that particular letter must be kept. After a time it will be possible to so word the mail shots that the response rate goes up. Clearly they can be timed with local events which would give them more impetus.

ADVERTISING

Advertising is what many solicitors appear to think marketing is about. Advertising is one of many promotional tools and is not particularly effective. It needs to be brief and to the point. It needs to be in the house colours and format and be positioned so that it gives the maximum impact.

Solicitors are quite the worst people to draft copy. Out comes the red pen and a fairly simple and punchy advert becomes a draft lease! It is probably as well to have an agency draft the advertisements for you. They can probably buy the space in the paper or magazines cheaper than you can, not least because they are placing copy all the time for a large number of clients. They will also ensure that you get the best position.

Remember to stop the advertisement from time to time. People get used to seeing the same advert and ignore it. People only take notice of advertisements when they are specifically looking for the product you are selling. For example, do you know what car is on sale today in your national paper? If you are thinking of buying a car you will know, but probably not otherwise. It is very easy to be persuaded to put your advertisement into a magazine or paper because all your competitors are doing the same. Sporadic advertising of that nature is a total waste of time. It must be geared to a marketing plan and be part of an overall strategy.

If you run an advertisement you must make sure that you monitor the results. This can be by alerting your reception and staff so that they can ask clients how they came to instruct the office. Alternatively you can request those responding to an advertisement to ask for a mythical member of staff. The reception can then keep a record of the number of calls asking for "Alice" or whatever the name is (make sure that everyone working in reception knows who "Alice" is!) They can advise that "Alice" is not available but that Margaret (the person actually dealing with requests arising from the advertisement) is available!

As explained above, it is not always necessary to use an advertisement to obtain newspaper coverage. For example if you a running a seminar there is no need to place an advertisement in the paper. All you need to do is write a short article telling readers what you have in mind and ask one of the feature editors if they will run it for you. If it is someone you know because you've taken them out for lunch, they will probably oblige. The paper might also be persuaded to come along and take a photograph of the event itself. If you give some sort of award at the event you might also get a photo-call for the next edition with a detail of how the seminar went. You will have achieved three advertisements at no cost and frequently in a form of which your clients approve.

INTERNET

The use of the internet in middle range practices is where the spreadsheets and word processors were ten years ago. It is going to grow substantially. The internet has already migrated in some practices from an on-screen brochure to an active supplier of information by clients interrogating the site. The more ambitious sites now take interactive form, able to disseminate legal information without the involvement of a partner or fee earner. The latter model can be currently very expensive to set up and needs a client base interested enough to pay a fee to the practice for the information: see page 163 for one option.

A website is of value but is principally for one's own clients. The chances of a third party addressing your site and then converting to a client cannot be high. However, in small provincial practices this may not be true if there is a definitive product which is user friendly and produces a positive result, provided the firm has advertised the service locally. Some firms use their websites for the preparation of wills. It is important to work out the cost and the likely number of "hits" to decide whether this sort of activity is worthwhile. Remember, if you are working on a 25% margin you need to turn over four times the cost of the website before you make a return at all. Even a fairly simple interactive site could cost over £6,000 to install. If it is to promote wills at £50 a time, it must generate 480 wills to achieve a 25% margin (£6,000 × 4 = £24,000/£50 = 480). Perhaps £6,000 could be put to better use in straightforward advertising?

SEMINARS

Seminars take a lot of organising and need fee earner time. They can be beneficial on several levels, however. First there is nothing like giving a lecture to make you understand how a subject works. It is therefore a useful learning curve for fee earners and partners alike. If the firm is registered with the Law Society for CPD points, it also enables other fee earners and trainees to accumulate their compulsory points. The seminar can be run as a commercial exercise, to make money as well as to highlight the competence of the firm. If it is open to the general public for a charge, some of those attending might well wish to instruct the practice. If it is being run as a marketing exercise for clients, it would make sense to ask other influential people to attend. They may never become clients but they will add a certain amount of credibility to the endeavour.

At the end of the seminar it is usual to arrange some refreshment and this is the opportunity to sell your services. If you ask other partners or staff to help, make sure that they know what is expected of them. If you can let the local press know, they will probably advertise it in an article for you and take photographs at the event for publication afterwards. That way you will have achieved the maximum publicity at the minimum amount of cost.

PUBLIC SPEAKING

Some partners or other members of staff may enjoy public speaking. If so, it might be a good idea to let organisations and clients know this as there is usually a dearth of after-dinner speakers. It is important that the partner or member of staff is skilled and if they are they will do the practice no harm by using their skill. There are many occasions when somebody is needed to make an address or help out with a charity. It does not matter that the person speaking is not necessarily involved with the client on advisory basis. As explained earlier, practices have to get away from the idea that clients belong to individual partners rather than to the whole firm.

MEETINGS AND NETWORKING

There are any number of opportunities to get out and about attending the promotional activities of other businesses. There are many different types of business clubs. It needs to be recognised that you are not attending these functions necessarily to get a new client, but more importantly to be seen around. If you can give votes of thanks or make presentations so much the better. You may well find that if you and your partners and fee earners are attending functions involving their particular expertise, work may well be generated from it. Even if it is not you will be keeping your ear to the ground and will have some idea as to what is happening in the marketplace. It is surprising how useful ideas can be triggered off by several stimuli from different sources.

CLIENT ENTERTAINING

This can take several forms. You can set up a specific venture, for example a wine tasting evening. It is a way for you to promote the practice to your clients and thank them for using you as their solicitor. These are also occasions at which you can get to know your clients better. Remember what has been said about seminars. These sorts of function must be carefully prepared. Think of the functions you have been to, particularly out of town. Have you ever walked into a room full of people who you do not know? Where nobody from the firm providing the function has bothered to greet you, let alone introduced you to a group you might like to meet? It is essential that you have "greeters". You must then have partners and/or fee earners who ensure that your guests have a drink and are introduced to a group. You then need to have partners or fee earners working the room to ensure that the people you want to impress or keep are properly looked after and told about those services you have to offer.

If there is to be a speech, make it short and to the point and if possible funny. If there are individuals within the partnership who are good at public speaking let them do it. Senior partners are not always the best people for job! Most importantly make sure that you contact the clients no later than two days after the event to see if they enjoyed it and to ask whether they need any specific advice.

It will be seen from the above that there is little point in running this sort of function unless it is well thought out and executed.

LUNCHES

It is surprising how few partners consider that it is necessary for them and their fee earners to invite clients out for lunch. This can provide a very pleasant break during the day and more importantly gives partners and fee earners the opportunity to get to know their clients better. If the conversations are addressed to the client so that he or she is persuaded to do all the talking, a great deal of information can be obtained. The added bonus is that the client will think that you are an ideal host as he or she will have talked about themselves for most of the time!

The perceived wisdom is that partners and fee earners should see at least four clients each month to promote the practice.

OUTSIDE ACTIVITIES

It might be that the firm has the use of a football box or executive suite. Alternatively it is always possible to hire football boxes, golf courses, racing days, etc. If any of these occasions are to be used it makes sense to take care about who you ask and for you to decide what the purpose of the event is. Most clients who attend will expect some sort of sales pitch! It is perhaps worth bearing in mind that there needs to be continuing efforts. Merely taking a non-client to a football match even to see his own team will not convert him to your business. If you are targeting a particular client or business you must be rather more subtle and persistent. It can take many months of hard graft to persuade a person to change their allegiance and even then they need to be dissatisfied with their present arrangements. It is perhaps as well that clients do not move too easily, otherwise a firm would lose its own clients as well!

SELLING

All marketing activity is designed to encourage existing clients to stay with the practice, so that they will recommend new clients, who in turn will do the same. There is little point in having a sophisticated marketing strategy if the leads so generated are not converted into work. This is why it is important to select the best people in the practice to carry out the promotion you have in mind. These people are not necessarily those you would expect. Mention has already been made of the reception and the telephone. It is quite likely that in many practices the work is allocated by the telephonist. It is no part of a telephonist's job description that they will know what a client needs if they are selling their business! It is necessary to select within each department an individual who can speak to existing or new clients in such a way that they will instruct the practice. Selling is a major subject in its own right. Prospective clients must feel at the first call that the firm can deliver all those "givens".

If the telephonist says:

> "I'm sorry there is no one in who can speak to you, can we ring back?", it is likely that an opportunity will have been lost.

Similarly if the secretary who next gets the call merely states a set price adding the inevitable words "if it's straightforward" the opportunity will again be lost. How do clients know if a matter is straightforward or not, particularly if they have never dealt with this sort of matter before? If you are to spend 2% to 5% of turnover on marketing, it is essential that somebody fields the enquiries generated properly.

The perceived wisdom is that if you can keep the client on the telephone for five minutes it is more than likely they will instruct you to act.

It is at this stage that you have to "close" the discussion. It is most important that the client is asked when they would like to make an appointment. Clients must feel that *they* are being given the choice in the matter. The whole tenor of the conversation at the end is to make clients feel that they want to instruct you, so that all the questions are addressed on the basis that they expect the answers to be positive. Surprisingly, these are skills that solicitors do not have, not least because they have not be trained in this way. Selling is not easy and needs a particular kind of person. The sale is by definition a soft sell. Solicitors are not being asked to sell double glazing. It would make sense, however, once you have the team of individuals who are going to man the front-line telephones to have them all trained!

The above list of marketing tools is not comprehensive, but is a sample of how one might go about promoting the practice.

How are you doing? Questions about your practice and departments

1. Do you have a marketing strategy?
2. Have you rung in to see how the receptionist copes?
3. Do you have you members of the firm who know how to handle new business opportunities?
4. Have you particular people you wish to attract as clients?
5. Have you run a seminar or function? If so, could you have done it better?
6. Does your advertising need looking at? Is it effective? How do you know?
7. Do each of the departments know what promotional activities the others are doing?

CHAPTER 9
MERGERS

"There is no way we can increase our fee income from organic growth. We will have to find a practice to merge with."

There are many reasons why firms want to merge but not all of them are properly thought out. PriceWaterhouseCoopers survey for 2000 reveals that 33% of firms believe that they will have to merge to achieve critical mass; 63% of firms with 50 partners and 80% of firms with over 80 partners are considering mergers. Among the smaller practices, most are looking for a firm of comparable size or smaller. Against that background some 50% of mergers either fail or fail to deliver their expectations.

There are several reasons why merging is difficult. Although solicitors are competent to advise their clients on the mechanics of a merger, they usually have insufficient information about their own firms to know exactly what they want for the new organisation. Change is not easy to handle at the best of times and given the perceptions and often hidden agendas behind the motivation to merge and the personalities concerned, not enough attention is paid to the human element of the merger. The parties fail to ask relevant in-depth questions about past performance and future aspirations. There is also quite frequently an inappropriate expectation as to timescales.

TYPES OF MERGER

There are several reasons why partners might want to merge. It may well be that with a decrease in margins, together with increased competition and salary costs, the only way to make a firm viable in the longer term is to achieve the perceived benefit of size. It is unlikely, however, that a successful firm would be looking to merge with a practice whose profit and loss account and balance sheet are starting to slide. The only basis on which such a merger might take place would in fact be a takeover by the stronger partner. That partner would then dictate to the smaller and less efficient practice what it wanted and there clearly some partners and staff would not be required.

A merger between two practices with similar falling profits and reducing balance sheets, would be unlikely to succeed. This is because the underlying problem as to the shape of the firms would continue and pure size is unlikely to solve that problem.

An aggressive and opportunist practice on the look out for further expertise or specialities might be able to persuade dissatisfied partners and staff to leave another practice. This is not really a merger situation. There have been several large exoduses from one practice to another, but the incoming group has usually been subsumed into a larger organisation. It is clear that deals have been struck, which must have left the in-coming group better off than they were with their former practice. They have, however, joined an organisation to which they will have to adapt.

The merger that is most likely to succeed is the one arising out of a carefully thought out business strategy, which has recognised that the only way to improve the services it gives to its clients, the security for the partners and staff and the bottom line profit, by merging with a firm with which it can created some synergy.

BUDGETARY REQUIREMENTS

In the first instance the individual practice must have a proper business plan. The partners must sit down and look not only at where the firm is but where it believes its market to be in future. All those matters which have already been discussed in Chapter 7 (strategic planning) have to be brought to the fore. Having established an appropriate shape, the partners must decide whether the business can grow organically, or whether it needs to go out into the market place to find a like-minded organisation that can help it expand in those areas where it believes its future growth lies. If the practice has decided on the likely size and mix of the target firm, it would make sense to prepare a draft financial model made up of the appropriate forecasts to achieve what is required. This would not only highlight whether the proposal is commercially sound, but also demonstrate the sort of shape that is being looked for in the target firm.

As the proposal forms part of the firm's business plan, it should have the consent of all the partners. There is no point in attempting to merge with another practice unless all partners agree in principle that a merger should be considered. Once the principle of merging has been established then when a target firm has been chosen, the partners need to be in agreement with that particular practice. On this occasion it may be necessary to agree that a majority decision of at least 75% of the partners would be sufficient for the merger to proceed. If there are partners who violently disagree, you can rest assured that down the track they will cause trouble or leave. It is therefore important to be aware of the needs of all the partners so that appropriate action can be taken as sympathetically as possible.

FINDING THE TARGET

Sometimes partners have contacts with other practices at a level which makes it possible for them to approach such partnerships. It needs to be recognised that the target practice might not have thought of merging. Undoubtedly they will initially be flattered by the approach, but it might take some time for all their partners to agree that the matter should be progressed. Whatever happens a strict timetable needs to be adhered to. It has to be made clear to the target firm from the first meeting that the offer is serious, otherwise a whole series of meetings will occur which do not really address the real problems and allow negotiations to become bogged down because the proposals have lost the initial impetus. This does not mean that there should be indecent haste, but there should be a determined effort to bring the proposals to a head.

NEGOTIATIONS

Assuming, however, that the first approach has generated some interest the next thing to do is to enter into a confidentiality agreement. It is accepted that a confidentiality agreement may not be enforced, merely because neither firm would want to become embroiled in heavy litigation. It is surprising how a confidentiality agreement concentrates the minds of the parties who sign them! It flags up to the other partners that the negotiations are for real, and they had all better get thinking about it.

It is at this stage that accounts need to be exchanged. It might be prudent to involve the accountants at this stage, unless a consideration of the accounts as presented reveals that a merger is not viable. The target practice's accounts may not be as sophisticated as those of the acquiring practice. This is probably because the acquiring practice has, as part of its merger strategy, got its own house in order. A careful consideration of the accounts is extremely important. Both parties will want to see several years' accounts and, if they are available, the management accounts for the current year.

First, both sides need to know, not only what the fees are but how they are made up. This means that the practices will need to be able to demonstrate the mix of their work. You then need to know how quickly the fees get paid. A full breakdown of the debtors is needed to see how long payment takes, and what the likelihood of bad debts might be. It will be recalled that the PriceWaterhouseCoopers report for 2000 reveals that a large number of firms still take more than 100 days to recover their fees. If the newly merged organisation is looking for say 50 days or less, then there is a danger that the clients of the target practice might move elsewhere, as they have been using the practice to accommodate their own cash flow. A gradual change of culture will be needed for those clients. Both sides must identify who their core clients are and make some initial judgement as to the likely effect of the merger on them. There is a suspicion amongst some clients that a merger is not for their benefit but is motivated by a desire to improve the bottom line.

DEBTORS

It is also worth asking how the fees are made up. As has been mentioned earlier (in Chapter 1), fee earners and partners can boost their fees by advance billing without submitting the bill to the client, or by adding to their bills work done by other fee earners which ought not to be credited to that particular fee earner or partner. A list of bills and disbursements outstanding with details of their age in months might be very revealing. If substantial sums are due to one or two partners or fee earners, it might well be that they will never be recovered at that level, with consequential effects on cash flow and pressure on the overdraft, if there is one.

PROPERTY

Property might become an issue. Some thoughts about property were raised in Chapter 4. While property can help the balance sheet, particularly if there is some borrowing, it can create real problems if one set of partners own the building and others do not. If the balance sheet can stand it, it might make sense to remove the properties and if they are to be used by the new organisation to consider a proper leasing arrangement. If that cannot be done then it is essential that the property should be professionally valued. Even better if the size of the new firm allows it, a new office should be acquired for the new organisation. The greatest benefit of this is that it places all the parties on the same footing when moving into the building. If one or other of the parties moves into an existing building it is very difficult in the short term for the newcomers not to be perceived as interlopers.

MARGINS

It is essential that the parties work out the margins for the various sources of work as described earlier. Fees alone do not identify the worth of a business. It is essential to know which parts of the firms are making a profit and at what level. If more than one branch is involved, it is important to know whether each of the branches is making a profit. This may not be immediately obvious if all branch accounts are consolidated. It is quite likely that the "principal office" is producing a true profit with contributions from individual branches. As the partners share the overall profit, the principal office may well be subsidising the branch-office partners' share. It would be important to deduct from individual branches the notional shares of their partners. For example, a branch office might be showing a profit of £45,000 generated by two partners. If their notional salaries should be £35,000 each, then this branch office is in fact £25,000 light in its contribution to overall profit (£70,000 − £45,000 = £25,000). If those two partners' share of the overall profits is actually £50,000 each, the partners in the practice as a whole are contributing, not £25,000 but £55,000. (The two partners' share of £100,000 profits, less the contribution from the branch office of £45,000). As we saw in Chapter 1 all the partners would expect to earn from the practice the equivalent to what they believe they could earn working for somebody else. If the branch or department does not produce enough profit to contribute to the notional salaries of the partners in the branch or department, other partners are going to have to make a contribution to those partners' share of profits. Even more important is to know if any are making losses. If they are, the same rules apply as running your own office. If they cannot be turned into profit-makers and are neither a loss leader for the work (wills for example) nor part of a new fee stream, then they should be closed down. It is quite likely that those departments which are showing high fees may not be as profitable as the top line would suggest. Often branch offices, although appearing to be making a profit are, after deducting notional salaries, making a loss. This might be acceptable in the short term for the purposes of the merger, but in the longer term the problem must be addressed.

CAPITAL ACCOUNTS

The capital accounts of the partners then require some thought. It is unlikely that both firms show the same capital structure. This will depend on the cultures as to debt within the practices. While there could be a very large variation, it seems from the PriceWaterhouseCoopers survey for 2000 that fixed capital typically represents 37% of all practices' funding, with current accounts representing 35%. If there is a very large discrepancy in the various capital accounts, it will be necessary to have an agreed basis for the division which is commercially viable. The problem with that might be that the very partners you want to merge with have capital accounts the adjustment of which are most complex. For example, they might have to borrow substantial sums of money to be on the same basis as the other partners. If the sum is too high, it might not be possible to fund the amount and the merge will founder. If, however, the partners can live with the position, they might be able to allow those capital accounts to grow by a reduction in drawings over the first few years.

The two firms' philosophies towards funding might be quite different. One practice might run a high overdraft with low fixed capital accounts and the other the reverse. Agreement needs to be reached in relation to overdrafts. 8% of capital funding appears to come from banks according to PriceWaterhouseCoopers 2000 survey. The partners need to be comfortable with what has been proposed.

WORK-IN-PROGRESS

Since the change in the legislation under the Finance Act 1998 all firms have to account for work-in-progress. It will be important to ascertain the relative positions of the two practices. If one has always accounted for work-in-progress and the other has only just amended its figures, it might be unreasonable to expect the other to pay the catch-up charge of the former.

Work-in-progress is valued in substantially different ways. According to the PriceWaterhouseCoopers 2000 survey, 50% of firms did not believe that they would need to make allowances for the catch-up charge. As PWC say, this is surprising, and when considering the merger it is important that you ascertain not only whether the catch-up charge applies but also on what basis work-in-progress is calculated. Of the firms surveyed, 17% had credited the additional work-in-progress to a central reserve.

OTHER CONSIDERATIONS

It may also be that the deal cannot get off the ground because pension arrangements, payments for goodwill and other benefits for retiring partners are incompatible.

MEETING THE PARTNERS

After the accounts have been properly studied and tested, it will be possible to decide whether the negotiations should continue. If they are, the next step is for the two sets of partners to meet each other. This should be exactly that. It should not be the occasion when detailed negotiations take place as to profit shares, the injection of capital or otherwise. It is difficult for people to get to know each other over such a short time. However, it is likely that several of the partners will know each other, certainly professionally (otherwise the merger proposals would never have got off the ground). If after that meeting there are no obvious clashes of personality then each side needs to agree a small team to sit down and thrash out the mechanics of the deal.

NET WORTH OF PARTNERS

It is probably at this stage that enquiry should be made of the net worth of the partners. This may lead to some difficulties but it is important to know if there are any partners with financial pressures. If so and the merged firm does not continue to make the profits the individual firms have made in the short term, there could well be difficulties relating to pressure on drawings balanced with the need to build up capital accounts. If the merged practice does not achieve the forecast profit in the first year, this will exacerbate the position.

DUE DILIGENCE

If no insurmountable problems have arisen to this stage, then the small group of partners from each practice can sit down and work out the mechanics of the merger. In the first instance it needs to be clear whether the negotiations are for a true merger or a takeover. If the former, which is the most likely to succeed, the parties must be careful when negotiating that they are not adversarial. It is worth remembering that "what goes round comes round"! There are plenty of areas for misunderstanding, that arise frequently from the difference in cultural matters.

The first and most obvious difficulty is the share of profits. It is unlikely that the shares in each firm are the same. It may not be possible to have equality from day one. It may be the practices recognise that in the longer term part of the profits may well be divided on the bases of a basic salary and an additional profit related to performance. The real difficulty, however, relates to the forecast and budget of the new practice. As has been mentioned earlier (Chapter 2) forecasts and budgets are always wrong. As a result, even allowing for a margin of error, it is unlikely the forecast profit will be achievable. The amount of productive time that partners and fee earners can achieve in a new environment will inevitable fall. This arises as a direct result of getting to know each other: the other firm's partners, fee earners and staff; and even getting to know one's way round the new office building and filing cabinets!

VARIATION IN ACCOUNTING PRACTICES

It is at this stage that the real variations in accounting procedures will come to light. It will be necessary to bring both firms into line. All the partners must be sensitive to each others' requirements. Those listening skills will need to be developed so that the minimum amount of damage is caused to sensitive egos. These will come to the fore not just at the agreement for the division of the profits, but more particularly in relation to the distribution of rooms. That, in itself, will be governed to a certain extent by the pecking order of the partners. Who is to be the senior partner? Is there to be a managing partner? How is the partnership to be run? These are difficult decisions and need very careful thought. As mentioned earlier in this chapter, personal and emotional perceptions are the hardest to evaluate. Some partners will be forceful and have no difficulty in saying what their expectations are. Others might be more diffident and appear to agree when really they are quite distressed. What all parties need to understand is that a merger is a permanent arrangement. It is not intended that the agreement should break down after the first year or two.

If there are partners or even members of staff who have not articulated their concerns, or worse whose concerns have been handled with scant regard, then there will undoubtedly be difficulties ahead. Further, you need only look at some of the high profile split ups of mergers, or failures to conclude them, to be aware of the turmoil that can occur.

COMMUNICATIONS

Investors in People encourages a dialogue between all parties in a structured and meaningful way. No doubt some considerable amount of lip service will be being paid to the system. This is best demonstrated in relation to the contracts of employment for the staff of each organisation. While it might be tempting to arrange that the best of each system will be used in the new organisation, this may not suit one or other set of staff. For example, holiday periods, particularly at Christmas; wage levels; bonuses and benefits in kind, will inevitably be different. It probably makes sense to give each set of staff the opportunity to sign up to the new contract, but if they are unwilling to, then to leave them on their existing contracts. Circumstances might require this as matter of law in any event. Three different sets of contracts may be messy, but they will work themselves out eventually and it is better to live with the differences than to create terrorists.

By whatever method the contracts are handled, it is imperative that senior staff become involved in the negotiations. Apart from assisting with practical matters of which the partners may not be aware, their involvement is essential to help them to own the change. After all if they have had a serious input into the negotiations they are going to make sure that their contributions have been worthwhile and work.

Inevitably it may not be possible to accommodate everybody and in those circumstances the parties should be honest and arrange to allow individuals to leave on as amicable a basis as is possible. You can rest assured that a nervous new workforce under the new arrangements will be very interested to see how you are going to deal with these matters.

TIME TO ADAPT

As with marketing and obtaining new clients, it takes a long time for the two firms to become subsumed into the new organisation. On a conservative basis it will take at least five years. There is therefore no need to do everything at once. In fact, if you attempt to do so, difficulties will arise. It stands to reason that the merger has been entered into for the mutual benefit of the partners and hopefully the staff in the longer term. Initially none of the parties involved will want to rock the boat. Everybody will try to accommodate each other and it will be some little time before individual staff team up with others whom they perceive to have a like perspective on life. Nobody can like everybody and by definition a merger creating a firm even as small as 15 partners will throw up personality difficulties. Inevitably there will be conflict and fairly fundamental disagreements before the new practice begins to develop. At some stage the concerns have to be addressed and healthy disagreement is a necessary part of growth and change.

There will be partners who have been looking for the opportunity to take up that judicial appointment. It is likely that everybody knows who they will be and have built their departure into the merger. In spite of the apparent agreement at the negotiation stage, there will be other partners and fee earners who will seek employment elsewhere because the merger has not achieved what they were looking for. On a less fundamental basis, the cultures of the two organisations will come to the surface and there will be clashes. This will undoubtedly be the case if the merger has not been properly planned.

SELF-INTEREST

There may have been partners who looked after their own interests rather than those of the partnership as a whole. This may have been on a departmental basis, in that they make sure that they get the best rooms, the new kitchens, etc. Such behaviour will build up resentment in others and when the opportunity arises they will make sure that the department does not get what it wants to the detriment of all.

The whole reason for the merger was an honestly held belief that the deal was beneficial for all parties. It would allow partners and fee earners to have the opportunity to develop their expertise. It would bring security and additional rewards for staff. If the deal was opportunist for one side or the other, it will inevitable become unstuck, or at worst create a working environment which is unpleasant.

It is impossible to get all these matters right but if there has been honesty from the beginning there should not be too many difficulties later on. Difficulties there must be, but if there is goodwill between the parties then they should not be insurmountable. If there is not, the merger will founder. It would be unfortunate if all that hard work, soft cost and emotion resulted in the practice breaking up.

How are you doing? Questions about your practice and departments

1. Are you contemplating merging?
2. If so what is the rationale?
3. Have you made all appropriate enquiries by way of due diligence?
4. Have you identified those matters which concern you and of which the others may not be aware?
5. Are there any signs that staff are genuinely concerned about the proposals?
6. If so is there anything you ought to be doing about it?

CHAPTER TEN
THE FUTURE

"I can't plan for twelve months ahead, never mind the future!"
Of course the Dodo had the same problem.

THE HISTORICAL PERSPECTIVE

This book addresses the issues of changing a practice into a business. Practices have always been businesses, but their managers have until recently always been solicitors. Business managers have been brought in, initially as practice managers. Many such practice managers have come from a commercial background and were not able to influence articulate owners as to the way they should be active and proactive in a business environment. As a result many of the practice managers have stopped trying and gone to work elsewhere.

Historically, the profession has not had reason to change. Clients were happy to instruct a solicitor and by and large pay their bills without too much difficulty. Net margins were running at 30% plus and managing the practice was not too difficult as there was plenty of slack in the system for mistakes to go unnoticed. The vision of the founder had become entrenched in a larger organisation running along much the same lines as previously. As a result management issues and procedures have become fixed. "We have always done it like this" was an adequate defence to most suggestions for change or growth.

Then came the recession. Much of the smaller end of the profession had become contented with the bulk of their work being conveyancing transactions, probate and some litigation. Even larger practices had developed cultures where money was no object, they had large prestigious offices, large motor cars, long lunch hours and extravagant entertaining.

Suddenly market share was under attack with less work around. What was the general reaction from the profession? It was to reduce the prices. Those who decided to tighten up their act, control expenditure and become effective and efficient at what they did, have survived and prospered. Others have seen net profit margins eroded from the 33% suggested as the original shape to 20% and falling. The only way to keep profits up is to work longer hours. Even so in many cases those firms are still allowing clients to pay late and possibly demand further reductions in the fees!

GROWTH AND SHAPE

It can be seen from what has been said above that standing still is not an option. This is because the marketplace insists on growth. Wages keep growing; staff expectations, as they move up the ladder, expand; new operators in the marketplace offer higher incentives to attract the high fliers to them. Pressure on fees has resulted in 1,600 productive hours or more becoming the norm. This is not peculiar to the large corporate organisations, but is replicated among the smaller legal aid practices that are trying to make ends meet and foster a social conscience, on an ever-diminishing revenue.

The only way forward is by growth, whether organic or by acquisition. The problem is, however, that most solicitors are not business people in the commercial sense. As they are running businesses, one or more of the partners must have an understanding of business processes and how to run a profitable business. They do not need to re-invent the wheel. Industry has been here before them and there are numerous books and courses on business management relevant to the profession. No solicitor would employ a corporate lawyer who knew very little about company law. No litigator would employ a personal injury solicitor whose only experience was making wills. Yet most of them, almost without exception, allow themselves to run a substantial business without any management training at all! The good old British tradition that "it will be all right on the night" will suffice. Unfortunately it will not in the current changing and competitive environment.

CORE BUSINESS

It is essential that the firm gets its shape right before it does anything else. No amount of change, growth, or acquisitions can be entertained until the practice is in the right shape. This means that the fee structure must be such that it can be sustained for a reasonable length of time (a minimum of five years) without coming under pressure. The expenses, wages, fixed and variable overheads must be sustainable to produce net profit; this must be sufficient not only to maintain the living standards of the partners but also to have the availability to fund any potential growth. Unless the practice has this shape it will not be able to sustain the growth it has in mind. The answer is of course to keep it simple. This is not rocket science and, like the barrow boy, need not be complicated. Individual departments must realistically examine their client base. They need to decide whether it is growing or shrinking. They need to honestly appraise where it might be going. It is no use having a strategic meeting which does not address the fundamental problems. The same department needs to look at the expenses and see how it can make itself operate within the desired shape (i.e. 25% to 30% margin).

SUPERIOR SERVICE

Even with the appropriate shape, growth will be easier to maintain if the way in which the business is carried out is correct. All the "kite marks" need to be in position to be used as standards and as useful business tools; that will ensure that work is being carried out efficiently and to the best advantage for the client. In this context the most expensive asset the firm has, namely the staff, must also buy into the proposals. If they are not properly informed and properly cared for, the platform will not be right to grow and more importantly to change direction.

COMMITTED ENTHUSIASM

Once the shape is right, ideally everybody has to genuinely buy in to the strategy and be committed to it. It is no use having a strategy, if one or more of the partners are going to pay lip service to it. At every opportunity they announce to their departments that it doesn't affect them. This effectively creates an atmosphere that will defeat any potential for growth and a lot of time and energy will have been wasted. It is unlikely that any change will take place unless at least 75% of the partners embrace the new ideas. Unless partners really accept that the only way forward is that devised from their strategic meeting, the impetus will be lost and the status quo will remain. Maintaining enthusiasm is not easy and can probably be achieved only by having an enthusiastic and enlightened leader. Such people are rare in partnerships. By definition partnerships are an amalgamation of varied abilities of which business management is not usually one. If you are fortunate enough to have such a partner, at whatever level, then encourage him or her, and send them on management courses. If you can allow them out of the office for some time to learn management skills, do so.

It is important that the firm operates to its best advantage. It is accepted that all this is a counsel of perfection, that most firms will not be able to achieve. There is no reason, why one should not go for the best targets, settling for second best is not acceptable. Clients would not be to happy if firms did!

CHANGE

It is worth remembering that change takes time. Businesses mature and decline. In order to survive in a changing environment, practices must sustain their growth. Partners need to focus their attention not only on the existing business but also on where they are heading. In *The Alchemy of Growth* Baghai, Coley and White describe this process as a pipeline. They suggest that core businesses are already out of the pipeline and operating as efficient profit generators. However, inside the pipeline are both emerging and future operations. Some developing services will already be showing promise and proving profitable, whereas the future operations are in their infancy and may only be good ideas, which have potential for future profit. The authors suggest that what distinguishes companies that sustain growth is their ability to create new business. These companies are able to innovate their core business while concurrently planning and building new ones. Unfortunately what seems to happen is that companies delay creating new businesses until it is evident that the core business is threatened and declining. At this stage competitors may have already moved in to the newer attractive areas.

What those new areas of business are is a matter of commercial judgement for each practice. Unless such judgements are made, there is every likelihood that the business will in the long term cease to be viable.

WHAT ARE SOME OF THE LIKELY CHANGES?

PRICING

The present method of costing legal work cannot go on for much longer. The purpose of time costing was always an in-house method of arriving at the price that the firm thought was reasonable for the work. The thought that in two to three years' time the clients will be told that the charge-out rate is £1,500 per hour is absurd. Apart from anything else it is not accurate.

Quoting prices on the basis of the value of the time needed to make the profits that the partners think they are entitled to, is suggesting to clients that some solicitors are making a lot more money than they actually are. There must be many small and middle size practices carrying on traditional legal work where the partners are earning less than £40,000 per annum and taking home a lot less than that because of the cash tied up in the business. The clients need to understand that a solicitor has to run an office, pay staff and overheads and make a profit for himself or herself. A bald statement that his or her charge-out rate is £225 per hour is meaningless. The client believes that the solicitor is taking home £225 per hour! On any showing it is not surprising that the public believes that solicitors are overpaid. The sensible way to show the take home pay is to identify the charge-out rate as a contribution to running the office, with a take-home figure at the bottom.

Your Rule 15 client care letter needs to identify that the fees are worked out on a time basis and are made up as follows:

- Hourly rate to cover the cost of the office, £175.50
- Balance available to partners, £49.50.

If criminal lawyers are working for 1,200 hours, their take-home pay will be £14,748. This is probably why any criminal lawyer worth his salt will join the prosecution service!

The only way to charge clients for much of the work in the future will be to quote a global price and stick to it. The only way that firms will know what that global price should be will be by continually keeping records of the bills delivered. Over a period of time practices will be able to assess their average prices for all their work. It is axiomatic that that the average price must be at an acceptable level. The firms will have to work out its in-house costs using the time costing calculations suggested in this book, so that it can be sure that their average price is viable.

Once the practice knows the average price, it can start charging the client on the basis of what it believes the client might pay, against a background of what they have been able to charge in the past. Where the work is specialised and the client is anxious to have it done quickly and accurately, it may be possible to charge more than for routine pedestrian work. If the average price for a commercial lease is say £1,200, the solicitor can charge more or less than that by making a judgement of how the client might react. The client has to be told at the start of the work in any event, so that it ought to be possible to sense what charge the client might find reasonable in all the circumstances.

The problem for the profession is that it is not currently allowed to haggle over its fees. If there is a regime in litigation, which allows the client to have a bill taxed or a remuneration certificate granted, there needs to be a system to show how a bill is worked out. Time costing lends itself to that system. Hence if the firm does not have a time costing system that accommodates the artificiality of taxation, they are going to be in difficulties if much of their work is currently calculated on the basis that it is going to be taxed.

The firm might in the longer term, from a commercial point of view, decide that it will not continue to provide litigation advice if the taxation procedure does not fit in with its strategy for growth. This is a line that many firms have adopted who were running legal aid practices.

Firms should not dispense with time costing but they should relegate it to a business tool and not a precise method of billing. If fees can be related to the average charge that the firm has made in the past, it would be a lot easier for the practice to know if it is going to make a profit. If the practice does not make what it believes to be a reasonable profit, it will eventually close down.

THE MARKETPLACE

Conveyancing fees during the recession persuaded clients that they could discount solicitors' bills. Once this principle was established it was used for other work. Hence in the city practices routine corporate work has suffered the same fate as conveyancing fees, since clients are aware that if they argue the fees might be reduced.

It is worse than that. Outside organisations who are not bound by traditional ways of doing things, have applied straightforward commercial ideas to the delivery of legal services. The profession has been slow to pick up on these activities and as John Harvey-Jones says in his book *Making it Happen*:

> "...one has to accept in life there is always at least an evens chance that one is going the wrong way. Not only is it extremely easy to go the wrong way, and indeed many businesses have foundered on the basis of one, usually inadvertent, mistaken direction, but all of us are aware that a lot of businesses aren't going anywhere at all. This is indeed the most dangerous situation of all. It is deceptively easy to keep busy maintaining the status quo, and belief in this function of management has been the source of decline of many proud company... you can be absolutely sure that, if that is the position in your business, somebody elsewhere has got your card marked as an easy number and is about to take you by surprise."

Licensed conveyancers are taking on traditional solicitors' work in-house for the larger building societies and estate agency chains. Commercial enterprises are linking into personal injury work by providing the infrastructure and more importantly the advertising and marketing clout. The major banks are making more wills (where they are appointed executors) than the entire profession is making.

The staple diet of conveyancing – personal injury work, wills and probate – are under attack. Several of the banks have huge will banks. Many practitioners are glad to move in-house to help the big boys develop their markets. The international practices will not have the same problem as the medium to smaller practices. They will, however, be subject to the market forces within their arena. Some city firms are already under pressure from the more commercially minded American practices in relation to salaries for their young lawyers. These are just beginning to bite into budgets.

PriceWaterhouseCoopers report for 2000 identifies that wages are now more than 40% of expenses and rising. Further, the need to open practices abroad in environments that partners do not necessarily understand can put a huge pressure on capital resource. If merging with an English firm is difficult, imagine what it is like doing so with one from a different culture with a different language and set of values.

COMPUTERS

The computer is here to stay and has not really been embraced by the profession. The principal reason for this is that solicitors do not see themselves as typists. Of course the younger breed of lawyer has no difficulty with that concept because the computer is only an extension of the "play stations". There is nothing demeaning in using a computer against that background!

The answer may be "voice", of course. The view on the street is that it will not catch on, but then neither did it think emails would five years ago. When we are all addressing our cars and domestic appliances through our mobile telephones, it will be no problem to talk to a computer.

The advent of the internet has put information which was sold at a premium by solicitors at the disposal of the client. In the not too distant future clients will have a fairly good grasp of the basic principles of general legal matters. Some of the profession (in an attempt to get market share) are already providing free documentation on the internet. The larger practices, with the ability to fund such exercises, are already providing bespoke legal advice, which can be accessed for an annual fee. This type of software is extremely expensive for the small to medium size practices. Perhaps the larger practices will make the packages available to smaller practices for a fee. Perhaps the price of the systems will eventually fall.

It is accepted that a lot of correspondence between solicitors still requires secretarial input to ensure that the right documents go with the right letters. It is likely, however, that advice and documentation will pass over the internet and not need to be made up at all. Clients will expect to address their files to see where the firm is up to. They might well leave messages to say what they want done next.

SKILLS

Some firms have already taken on the challenge of the internet and computers. PriceWaterhouseCoopers 2000 report reveals that in 5% of practices at least 2% of turnover is now done through the internet.

At the turn of the last century no man of property would be seen without his lawyer. Maybe that is the way the profession has to go. The men of property these days are the companies and larger corporations. They are quite able to deal with pedestrian matters of law but are undoubtedly looking for the specialist.

The way to develop must be to play to these skills. Specialisation has to be the key. Arbitration and ADR are up and coming, as is mediation. Taxation, trusts and complicated commercial transactions will always require a quick mind. More esoteric areas of law: intellectual property, patents and computer law, must be specialist areas that can command a premium rate. After all there is very little point in spending eight years learning the law, to end up doing something a non-qualified person can easily master.

It is for these reasons that partners must have strategic planning sessions and allow a free flow of ideas. Lateral thinking coupled with a thorough understanding of the market place must give solicitors the edge when it comes to taking opportunities. The problem is that moving out of one's comfort zone is not easy. It is far easier to stay with what you know even if it is disappearing. If you have been "running the numbers" as outlined in this book it will have become clear what areas of work are becoming unprofitable and the likely timescale before they must be replaced. Similarly with strategic planning, firms can take on board new ideas which may begin to bear fruit.

THE WORK PLACE

Although there is no doubt that the computer will and is taking over our lives, it is unlikely that it will take over entirely. Some of the gloss has already gone off the technology markets with questions being asked as to their ability to make money. It is certain that a lot of menial tasks will be taken up by computers and that much basic law and business will become a "given". Fortunately human beings need human contact and although there will undoubtedly be more working from home using the internet or an intranet for the connection, people will want to meet from time to time. They will want to catch up on their technical skills with an interchange with their colleagues. They will undoubtedly want to catch up on the gossip!

Two things might develop, however. The first is that work time will be, and is already, becoming more flexible. Pieces of work will still have to be done by a given time, but with the advent of instant communication there is no reason why the work should not be done when and where it suits the employee and down-loaded to a central computer when it is needed. The other consequence of that flexibility is that there will be less need for office space. Offices will be available on a 24-hour basis and as a result the capital employed will be far more efficiently utilised. Office space will be shared as will the technology, so that three or four people can operate from one station. This will have the effect of reducing the rental on office accommodation as there may well be an over-supply. Alternative it will put a premium price on office space appropriately equipped to deal with a high-tech environment on a 24-hour basis.

Office work which can be accessed either at the office or from home by way of mobile telephones down-loaded to computers opens up all sorts of possibilities. One of the greatest attractions is that overhead costs will go down. Further, this will enable practices to become more competitive by passing on the saving to the client, or even better keeping more of the bottom line for themselves!

CLIENT BASE

Even though the computer is here to stay, many firms do not have sophisticated databases. Those that have are starting to use them as a management tool. Far too frequently firms do not contact their existing clients after the current piece of work has been completed believing that they will return automatically. This might have been so 20 years ago but it is by no means certain these days. People have short memories and often firms are no better than their last job. If there is a database which not only contains the names of the clients but also the types of work handled, it would be sensible to have some form of communication with that client base on a regular basis. Such communication would keep the name of the firm before the clients. More importantly, if the firm has in fact taken time to learn something about the client the last time they met, then it would be able to alert the client to changes in the law relevant to that client.

CONCLUSION

Solicitors have a substantial training in the law and are articulate and intelligent people. None of the matters raised in this book is complicated and their implementation should enable practices to take advantage of the opportunities which abound. The profession needs to apply the skill and care it gives to its clients to the management of its practices. Whether firms like it or not, practices are businesses and need to be run as such. A solicitor's culture may be professional, which means that the interests of the client must always come first, but that does not mean that they should abandon all busines techniques. Solicitors need to accept that they are running businesses and they will succeed only if they go for the best. There is no reason why all of us cannot "raise our game"!

How are you doing? Questions about your practice and departments

1. Is your core business producing enough profit for you to grow?
2. Our your margins rising or falling?
3. Has your market share grown?
4. Have you any new services in the pipeline?
5. If so how developed are they and is it worth your while investing further in them?
6. Has your leadership team set aside enough time to consider new opportunities?

FURTHER READING

Adair J, 1996, *Effective Motivation* (Pan Books), ISBN 0330344765

Baghai M, Coley S, White D, *The Alchemy of Growth* (Texere Publishing Ltd)

Beardwell I, Holden L, 3rd Edn 2000, *Human Resource Management. A Contemporary Perspective* (Prentice Hall), ISBN 0273643169

Blanchard K, Johnson S, 1994, *The One Minute Manager* (Harper Collins), ISBN 0006367534

Gormley G, *Practical Pricing* (Leading Lawyers, London), ISBN 0953098508

Handy C, 1990, *Inside Organisations* (BBC Enterprises), ISBN 0563208309

Harvard Business School *Harvard Business Review on Change* (Harvard Business School Press), ISBN 0875848842

Harvey-Jones J, 1994 *Making it Happen* (Harper Collins), ISBN 0006383416

Makin P, Cooper C, Cox C, 1989, *Managing People at Work* (British Psychological Society & Routledge Ltd), ISBN 1854330101 (paper), 185433011X (hard bound)

PriceWaterhouseCoopers, *Financial Management in Law Firms Survey 2000*

Robbins S H, Finley M, *Why Teams Don't Work* (Peterson's/Pacesetter Books)

Stewart I, Joines V, *T A Today. A New Introduction to Transactional Analysis* (Lifespace)

Underwood K, *No Win No Fee* EMIS P.P. 2001 185112167

West M, Creativity and Innovation at Work, *Psychologist*, Vol 13, No. 9, 460–464

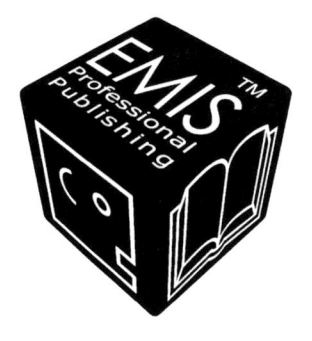

EMIS SERVICES TO THE SOLICITOR'S PROFESSION

EMIS Professional Publishing is part of EMIS Legal, which provides a wide range of software and publishing solutions for the solicitor's profession. Identify your need and see what EMIS has to offer!

This page: software *Next page*: hardware and publishing.

COMPUTER SOFTWARE

At the heart of EMIS Legal is the Seneca family of products:

best seen at www.emislegal.com. Priced in such a way as to be affordable for the smallest practice, Seneca software is the future!

SenecaWeb for an interactive website designed by lawyers that costs as little as £695 + VAT!

Seneca CM Legal Case Management System is a full 32-bit Windows application, designed to combine functionality with ease of use. Advanced, flexible and versatile, Seneca CM utilises industry-wide open standards such as XML technologies. The web browser style, intuitive interface facilitates speed of access to and input of data. Naturally, Seneca CM incorporates a task list and diary note facility, automatic document and form generation, data merge, legal spell checker, direct links to e-mail, the ability to export/import facilities to any file format, or embed objects including multi-media. The Attachments module allows bulk scanning of multiple documents, and any Windows file can be attached to the client file. Seneca CM integrates seamlessly with Microsoft® Word and Excel.

Seneca KM is both document management system and a knowledge management system. A *document management* system essentially holds relatively simple information about a document - for example the author's name, when the document was created and what type of document it is (whether it is a letter, fax, lease, etc). This can be used with a simple search engine to retrieve documents. Document management then goes beyond that into controlling/managing the process of creation and maintenance of templates and documents that go through many versions. *Knowledge management* software goes beyond even that into providing sophisticated tools for creating and managing the underlying knowledge implicit in the documents establishing deep links in the text (whether direct links e.g. a search for 'snail' returns all documents containing the word 'snail' or conceptual e.g. a search for snail also returns gastropods and even cases on the law of negligence).

SenecaIntranet The implementation of an Intranet will facilitate a fast, secure means of dissemination of knowledge between users. An internal network system, Intranets are ideally suited to help manage internal administration and provide a platform for Practices, Clients and others (e.g. counsel, estate agents) to communicate, standardise and present information. SenecaIntranet does this...and integrates with other Seneca products.

Contact tel: (08701) 225 525   www.emislegal.com

COMPUTER HARDWARE

Egton is one of Europe's largest dealerships and, as part of EMIS, we can offer lawyers exceptional prices on all forms of IT hardware and support.

Contact tel: 08701 215 215   www.egton.net

PUBLISHING FOR MANAGEMENT

Litigation
No Win No Fee	Kerry Underwood – 2001 £38	Making conditional fees work in practice cashflow and marketing examined.

Accounts
Credit Management for Law Firms	Julia Walden 1999 £38	Practice and procedure for better cash collection

Marketing
Solicitor's Manual of Marketing	Ian Cooper 2001 £275	Looseleaf collection of precedents, with commentary on advertising and marketing materials
How to Get the Fees You Deserve	Ian Cooper 2001 £49	Marketing to maximise fees
Marketing to Existing Clients	Ian Cooper 2001 £49	Materials and ideas to maximise cross-selling

Skills Audio Tapes
Effective Time Management	Tony Hackett 1999 £45+VAT	Making the most of time for fee-earners and staff alike.
Effective Telephone Skills	Tony Hackett 1995 £36+VAT	For staff training on telephone skills.
Effective Presentation Skills	Avril Carson 1996 £42 + VAT	Aimed at solicitors who wish to develop their professionalism in presentations.

Contact: Rob Owen 01707 334823   www.emispp.com

INDEX

Accountancy, 28
Accruals, 71,79
Administrative wages, 27
Advertising, 5,29,123,132
Appraisals, partners, 110
Appraisals, staff, 108
Audit, 28
Average time to pay, 44,56

Bad debts, 30,57
Balance sheet, 4,63-80
Banking costs, 31,49,53
Billing in advance, 13
Billing late, effect of, 19
Branch office, management charge, 30
Break-even, 12,14
Budget
   Preparing, 22-42

Capital accounts, 53-54,63,75
   Mergers, and, 144
Cash flow, 4,43-61
   Forecast, 33
      Bad debt, 57
      Capital accounts, 53
      Disbursements, 57
      Drawings, 53
      Expenses, 48-49
      Fees, 44,45
      Income tax, 54
      Motor, 55
      Receipts, 48
      Seasonal variation, 48
      VAT, 46,55
   Increasing importance, 8
Change, future, 154-159
   Pricing, 154
Charge rates
   Calculating, 3
   Time basis, 8
Charge-out rates, 8
   Clients, and, 9
Client account, 49
Client meetings, 128
Client records, 127,159
Client surveys, 128
Committees, 96,100
Communication, 101
   Breakdown, 102

Computers, 4,81-94
   Backup and storage, 88
   Definitions, 81
   Future, 157
   Internet, 90
   Networks, 87,89
   Strategy, 92
   Training, 85
   Updating, 85
   Voice recognition, 86
Conditional fees, 43,57
Confidentiality agreements, 141
Contribution, 11
Conveyancing fees, 7,15,16
Cost drafting, 26
Costs *see* Expenses
CPD *see* Training
Creative thinking, 100
Creditors, 70-73,79
   Hire purchase/lease, 74
   Long-term creditors, 74
   Overdraft, 73
   Taxation, 71
   VAT, 72
Cross-selling, 126
Current assets, 66-70
   Debtors, 67
   Prepayments, 70
   Work in progress, 66,79

Data processing, 26
Database, 127,159
Debtors, 67,79
   Mergers, and, 142
Department, managing, 101
Departments, teams, and, 98,100
Depreciation, 29
   Cash flow, and, 53
   Goodwill, 66,79
   Tax and, 71
Direct costs, 23-27
Disbursements
   Cash flow, 57
   Outstanding, 67
Discounting bills, 19
Drawings, 53,54,75-76
   Overdraft, and, 73

Email, 90
Entertaining, 24
   Marketing, 30

Equipment leasing, 25
Equipment repairs, 26
Establishment costs, 28-31
Expense of time, 8
Expenses, 22-42
    Cash flow, and, 48-49
    Percentage, as, 21

Fees
    Allocation, 13
    Cash flow, 44
    Departmental analysis, 35
    Forecasting, 31-33
    Mergers, and, 142
    Per solicitor, 12
Finance costs, 31
Fixed assets, 63-66
    Fixtures and fittings, 64
    Goodwill, 65
    Motor vehicles, 65
    Office equipment, 65
    Premises, 64
Fixed cost, 11
Fixtures and fittings, 64
Flexible working, 159
Forecasting, 4 *and see* Budgeting
Future, 151-160

Goodwill, 65-66
    Depreciation of, 79
Green form, 9
Gross profit, 11
Gross profit margin, 22

Hackers, 91
Hire purchase/lease, 74

Income tax, 54-55
Indirect costs 27-28
Indemnity insurance, 28
Inflation, 22
Innovation, 100
Interest, client account, 49
Interest, set-off, 31,49
Internet, 4,90,157
Investors in People (IIP), 4,26,103,106,107-108,147
ISO standards, 4,26,103,106
IT strategy, 92

Leases, accounting for, 65,74
Legal aid, 9

Franchise, 106,107
Lexcel, 4,26,103,106,107
Library, 29
Liquidity, 74-76,79
Listening, 102
Litigation, cash flow and, 48
Long-term creditors, 74

Mailshots, 132
Management by committee, 96
Management culture, 106
Management structures, 95-112
Management of people, 95-112
Management charge, branch office, 30
Marginal cost, new staff, 27
Managing, departments, 101
Managing partner, 97
Managing staff, 97
Managing teams, 99
Margins, 32,143
Market, the future, 156
Marketing, 5,29,123-137
    Benefit-driven, 128
    Client records, 127
    Client surveys, 128
    Cross-selling, 126
    Implementing strategy, 123
    Objectives, 129
    Premises, 125
    Price, competing on, 128
    Priorities, 126
    Promotional activity, 130
        Advertising, 132
        Articles, 130
        Brochures, 130
        Client entertaining, 135
        Internet, 133
        Lunches, 135
        Mailshots, 132
        Meetings, 135
        Networking, 135
        Newsletters, 131
        Other activities, 136
        Public speaking, 134
        Radio, 131
        Seminars, 134
    Selling, 136-137
    Service delivery, 124
    Staff, 124
    Style, 125
    Telephone/reception, 125
Mergers, 5,139-149

INDEX

Accounting practices, 146
  Budgetary requirements, 140
  Capital accounts, 144
  Communications, 147
  Contracts of employment, 147
  Debtors, 142
  Due diligence, 145
  Finding the target, 141
  Margins, 143
  Meetings, 145
  Negotiations, 141
  Net worth of partners, 145
  Property, 142
  Self-interest, 148
  Types, 139
  Work-in-progress, 144
Mission statements, 119
Mistakes, allowing for, 103
Motor expenses, 30,55,65

National Insurance Contributions, NIC, 39
New staff, marginal cost, 27
No win no fee *see* Conditional fees
Notional partner salary, 8,23

Objectives, management, 103
Office equipment, 65
Open-ended funding, 53
Outstanding fees, 56
Overdraft, 73,79

Partner appraisal, 110
Partner away days, 116
Partnership deed, 95
Payment days before, no, 44
Pension provisions, tax and, 54,72
Performance, appraising, 108
Postage, 25
Practising certificates, 25
Praising, 105
Premises, 64,125
Prepayments, 70
Price, selling on, 128
Pricing, 7-20 *and see* Charge rates
  Future, 154
Printing, 25
Private health, 26
Probate, cash flow and, 28
Productive hours available, 15
  Effective of increasing, 16
Profit, 11

Target, 21,119
Profit and loss account, 63-80
Promotional activity, 130
  Advertising, 132
  Articles, 130
  Brochures, 130
  Client entertaining, 135
  Internet, 133
  Lunches, 135
  Mailshots, 132
  Meetings, 135
  Networking, 135
  Newsletters, 131
  Other activities, 136
  Public speaking, 134
  Radio, 131
  Seminars, 134
Property
  Mergers, 142
  Revaluation, 31
Publications, 29

Quality standards, 4

Reception, 125
Remuneration certificates, 18
Rentals, 25
Reprimanding, 104
Revaluation of property, 31,79
Risk management, 28
Rule 15, 19,68,155

Scanning, 84
Selling, 136-137
Seminars, 134
Service, superior, 153
Set-off, interest, 31
Shape, business, 1,2,5,12
  Future, 152
  Mergers, and, 140
  Solicitors' practice, 13-18,21
Solicitor's indemnity insurance, 28
Spreadsheets, 86
Staff, management of, 4,97,153
Staff appraisals, 108
Staff meetings, 98
Starting a practice, 3
Stationery, 25
Strategic planning, 5,113-122
  Action plans, 120
  Compiling the plan, 117
  Future trends, 122

Goals, 119
Identifying strengths and weaknesses, 117
Identifying threats and opportunities, 117
Identifying trends, 115
Stroking, 105
Subscriptions, 25
Sundries, 25
Super profit, 3,8,11

Tax *and see* Income tax
   Current liability, as, 71
   Depreciation, and, 71
   Pensions, 54,72
   Work in progress, 66,67
Taxation of costs, 18
Team meetings, 98
Teams, 95-112
   Composition, 100
   Reasons for failure, 100
Telephone, 24,125
Temporary staff, 24

Time recording, 8,9
Total assets, 74
Training, 26
   Computer, 85
Travel expenses, 24
   Marketing, 30
Turnover, 10,11,12

Underperformance, 105

Valuation, practice property, fees, 31
Variable cost, 11
VAT, 46,55,72
Viruses, 91
Voice recognition, 86

Wages and salaries, as percentage, 21,23,33
Websites, 90,133,162
Word processing, 83
Work in progress, 66,79
   Mergers, 144
Writing off bad debts, 57